COMPASSION
IN ACTION

COMPASSION IN ACTION

My Life Rescuing Abused and Neglected Animals

SCOTLUND HAISLEY

With Richard Folkers

SKYHORSE PUBLISHING

Skyhorse Publishing books may be purchased in bulk at special discounts for sales promotion, corporate gifts, fund-raising, or educational purposes. Special editions can also be created to specifications. For details, contact the Special Sales Department, Skyhorse Publishing, 307 West 36th Street, 11th Floor, New York, NY 10018 or info@skyhorsepublishing.com.

Skyhorse® and Skyhorse Publishing® are registered trademarks of Skyhorse Publishing, Inc.®, a Delaware corporation.

Visit our website at www.skyhorsepublishing.com.

10 9 8 7 6 5 4 3 2 1

Library of Congress Cataloging-in-Publication Data is available on file.

Cover design by Rain Saukas

Print ISBN: 978-1-63450-570-3
Ebook ISBN: 978-1-63450-973-2

Printed in the United States of America

This book is dedicated to those who wait for justice and an end to their suffering. May they soon be wrapped in arms of compassion.

CONTENTS

INTRODUCTION

The relationship between humans and animals has evolved throughout history. Academics may debate who domesticated whom, but in the twenty-first century, most people embrace the companion animals they call pets as family members. Companion animals are fortunate. Most people view other animals as a source—of food, entertainment, raw materials like leather, additives to cosmetics, and more.

Debates about how we currently treat animals and how we should treat animals will, I believe, lead to ever-more equitable treatment of animals globally. The number of those practicing compassion with their choices and actions will grow and inspire others by example.

The portion of the world I work to change every day is one where compassion for animals is missing. I have dedicated my life to forgotten, abused, and neglected animals, animals who suffer in tiny, dark enclosures with no companionship, no veterinary care, and often without edible food or clean water. I work with law enforcement agencies to close down places of abuse—one at a time. I am deeply honored to make this my life's work.

My purpose on these pages is to expose you to my world and enlist your help to change it—to create the world we want to see. I hope this book will inspire positive change in your daily life and encourage you to be part of the greater solution. And if you see animals being abused or neglected, please contact your local authorities and/or report the situation to Animal Rescue Corps at reportcruelty@animalrescuecorps.org.

Thank you.

CHAPTER ONE

OPERATION
UNBRIDLED SPIRIT

When you get close to one, you can almost always smell a puppy mill. It's an odor you remember. Not a pleasant memory, like the irresistible, wafting scent of a freshly bathed family dog drowsily nuzzling against your chest. This smell is ever so slightly sweet but acrid and nauseating, a nose-piercing vapor emitted by piles of accumulated, rotting feces that have been marinating for weeks or months, if not years, in urine that has decomposed to become ammonia, a colorless gas with a particularly pungent smell. It clings to your nostrils. It's a smell that, once experienced, you can conjure at will—in the same way you might remember, perhaps, the sulfur stench of a stink bomb released in a school cafeteria, the chlorine that permeates the air around a swimming pool, or the sterilized, medicinal smell of a hospital ward. Ammonia is a smell of decay and death.

As we drive the last few blocks to the house in Wayne County, Kentucky, on a muggy Thursday morning in late September, there is just a hint of the telltale odor that betrays this place. What we come upon is just a rundown, nondescript house on a country road, with a front façade largely obscured by untrimmed trees and shrubs. A pickup truck, a van, and a camper trailer are parked in the driveway, in front of a cluttered carport. As our caravan, led by police and emergency vehicles, drives onto the property, up the sloping driveway, there is nothing about the house or its yard that offers a clue to its nature—save for the small, stenciled sign out front that reads "Taylor's Kennel" and, above it, a street sign that says, "Kennel Ln." Although I have never before visited this property, it is much like dozens, if not hundreds, of similar places I have been, escorted by law enforcement.

My team and I wait in the driveway as a detective knocks on the front door, shouting "Sheriff's Department." His knocks continue and grow louder—pounding overhand with the fleshy part of his fist—over the next five or six minutes. Finally, a man wearing nothing but a pair of denim shorts emerges. He looks to be in his sixties; his most notable feature is a large, gray, walrus-like moustache. Moments later, a slender blonde woman of about the same age, wearing what look like plaid pajama pants and a blue, short-sleeved top, appears, a cigarette dangling from her lips. With the county attorney just a few feet away, the detective and his sheriff step inside the house, where, according to plan, they explain to the woman details about a seizure warrant I am about to help them execute. With some barking in the background and more of the telltale smell beginning to waft out, we are mere minutes away from verifying, with our eyes, that this is, in fact, a puppy mill, a dog factory hell.

I have to suppress my nerves. It isn't anxiety born from fear that I will encounter scenes of suffering. I've done that hundreds of times before. I sweat the details because I rescue animals, and my team and I must do everything right. We are spending the money of our donors, and we are potentially risking the trust and credibility of a community's justice system. If a criminal case falls through, if conditions are not clearly in violation of the law, if someone gets bitten or seriously hurt, if an animal is injured, it's my problem. The reputation of my organization, Animal Rescue Corps, is on the line. It was my people, our investigation, my urging, and my assurances that brought us here. A mistake or a misjudgment jeopardizes our ability to rescue abused animals tomorrow, next week, and beyond. I live for this work, and I can't afford to screw it up. Lives depend on me.

Especially in the south, what we have to offer communities is unique and often alien to them. Yet rescuing suffering animals also requires me to focus, in the moment, only on their well-being and not focus on any other agendas, meanings, or missions.

When I founded Animal Rescue Corps, I rededicated myself to a mission as straightforward as our fledgling group's name. Over the years, I have headed up the animal rescue team for the Humane Society of the United States. I ran and redesigned what is still considered the model of humane animal shelters. I have held leadership positions protecting animals in Manhattan, the San Francisco Bay Area, and Washington, DC. Animals are my passion; protecting them is my business, and saving them is my life. Doing well—satisfying my passion and my profession—requires that I approach each case, each puppy mill, each situation of abuse, with clinical seriousness. There is a time for emotion. There is a time for philosophy and sentiment. First we have to make a case.

The puppy mill owner's Facebook page, which was removed shortly after the raid, contained posts and pictures about Christmas and Christian faith, along with preciously decorated pictures of litters of pups. Information alongside some of the images specified dates when the dogs would be available for purchase. The caption on one picture proclaimed, with a certain license for unique spelling, spacing, and punctuation, "Ihave7 new babbys,," Her ad on a dog breeders' website, now also removed, said, "Raised with lots of lovin'!" Touting her twelve years of dog breeding experience, it added, "Puppies are handled daily with lots of tender love & care. Our pups make great family pets and are good with kids." It turned out there was neither tenderness nor care. As to whether there was love, it was certainly not evident in what we found.

The case that brought our team to this house began, as so many do, with a tip. An animal activist, someone new to us, from nearby in Kentucky had heard rumors and had visited the property under the guise of shopping for a puppy. She left appalled. Before looking to us at Animal Rescue Corps, she had contacted the Humane Society of the United States and People for the Ethical Treatment of Animals. She contacted Wayne County Animal Control, as had PETA, which was organizing resources to start a shaming campaign using social media, to demand action from local officials. We asked PETA to stand down. Too often, when people learn of a potential case, rather than just going straight to us, they go to lots of people, assuming that the best course of action is to involve every animal welfare organization they can name. That's a problem. It's all the worse when they go to Facebook or Twitter, trying to create pubic scorn. Unfortunately, most of the time, that's what they do first, believing that making noise will make change. A cast of thousands of advocates or a thousand social media posts will not help make a case. When you make noise to a sheriff's department, the first reaction of law enforcement officials is usually to defend and strike back. This kind of shaming is ineffective. It's an in-your-face process to which I am opposed. When we get a legitimate report, the first thing we say is, "Stop talking. Stop posting. Don't do anything. Lets us look into it. We'll get back to you."

After some initial research, we embraced the Kentucky informant and asked her if she could get back on the property. We sent one of our seasoned investigators from Tennessee to accompany her. Armed with a cellphone camera and video cameras disguised in sunglasses and a shirt button, they posed as workmates, one advising the other on what dog to buy. Their words and images were explicit demonstrations of suffering and cruelty. We bolstered their report, bringing in our general counsel, Alicia Pell, who added her analysis of state and local ordinances she alleged were being violated. Dr. Heather Robertson, our veterinarian for this case, added medical opinions based on what she saw in the still photos and video.

The fifty-eight-page document and supporting electronic files walked through documentation of approximately seventy dogs, several birds and cats, and possibly some miniature horses on the property—numbers we knew from experience may not have been comprehensive but that represent numbers the investigator saw. It cited a list of deficiencies that could be a template for what you find at a puppy mill: inadequate food, water, shelter, and veterinary care. Our undercover investigators reported and documented parasites, emaciated bodies, hair loss, and severe matting; dogs covered with feces; and a prominent ammonia smell.

Just a few days after we heard about this puppy mill, I headed for Kentucky with their report in hand.

Wayne County is rural country marked by rolling hills and rugged mountains. It has a population of about 21,000 and a median family income of about $25,000, about half the national average. It is a landscape dotted by small towns and signs for places like the Jesus Name Tabernacle. It may not be my natural habitat, but I also know from experience that there is great peril in underestimating the knowledge and abilities of local officials we are about to meet.

But where do we start? Do we go the sheriff or animal control, to a rank-and-file police detective, or to the local prosecutor? Or do we go above all of their heads, to regional or state officials? It's a judgment call and, frankly, we have to go by hunch and gut feeling as much as anything. What we do know from experience, though, is that most people appreciate being the first to know about something that's under their purview. No one likes being handed a case file and told, "Here, go do this." In this situation, my hunch was correct. I started with the animal control officer.

When a report is ready, I jump. If an informant gets antsy and decides to take matters to social media, a lot of work can go down the drain. Even worse, a puppy mill operator might get tipped off. I had been about to head home to Washington, DC, from Indiana, where I had been assessing a local shelter, but as soon as I signed off on the Kentucky investigation report, I booked a flight to Nashville instead. I called our investigator and asked if she was available to meet the next day, September 12. That morning, she picked me up from the airport, and we made the three-hour drive to Monticello, Kentucky. At this point, we had not been in touch with local officials—by phone, email, fax, or any other method. I placed my first call to animal control when we were just thirty minutes away. "I'm Scotlund Haisley from Animal Rescue Corps," I said. "I've just flown in to talk to you about an animal cruelty case in your community."

The animal control officer wasn't too crazy about that: Some guy he'd never heard of from some organization he'd never heard of just planned to show up. Typically, when you call local authorities about an animal cruelty case, they want you to hand over every detail right away, even if just verbally. If you have a written report, they want you to send it by email or talk it through on the phone but not bring it. They don't want you showing up on their doorstep. When you come in person, you are implying action, immediate action. Reached by phone, the Wayne County animal control officer said he was out on a service call and wouldn't be available for a while. I said I would wait.

Animal control is in a brick-and-block building labeled "Wayne County Road Department Office." The pound—a particular kind of place we will discuss later—consists of six cages in a carport out back. William Hale, the animal control officer, is a graying, mustachioed Kentuckian, who clearly values someone who gives him facts and looks him squarely in the eye. He sees a handshake as a bond. That's important, because what we do and what we have to offer someone like Hale is unheard of. You have a group spending tens of thousands of dollars—an amount that can easily eclipse a small community's entire annual budget for animal control—parachute into your community and resolve for you a problem with animals that you might not have been aware of. You must be a crazy animal rights group with an ulterior motive, they think—which means the first challenge is to demonstrate that we are professionals and not crazies. It starts with our demeanor and seriousness, but when we hand over an exhaustive report, they get serious. We know what's needed.

I sometimes compare presenting a report to cooking. If you are, ✗ say, a vegan and you will be serving a meal to someone who is not a vegan, you are under quite a bit of pressure. Your approach to food is different and perhaps threatening, and simply because it is different you may be perceived as challenging tradition. The meal you are about to serve needs to be convincing. It needs to be flavorful and appetizing. To persuade someone to take seriously something alien, you must serve him or her only the best you have to offer. So it is with an animal cruelty report in a place where I have no relationships. I am getting to know people and a situation, even as I am asking local officials to trust me and then, together, take on an outsized task.

My impromptu, ambush meeting with Hale stretched to half a day and moved to the office of county attorney Thomas Simmons, the person with the power to make this rescue proceed or come to an unceremonious end. A sandy-haired bear of a man, he was sitting in a large, carpeted office behind an imposing oak desk, with a wall full of law books at his back. The most striking decorations in the office all related to duck hunting: painted wooden ducks, decoys, trophies, and pictures. A shotgun shell bandolier was draped around the legs of a table. Simmons didn't rise to shake my hand, nor did he give me more than a passing glance. It was a gesture of authority I've seen before. I proceeded to lay out our investigation, hoping he would see my presentation as a case about the law and not about a philosophical point of view. My word choices are important. I don't lie about who I am, but I need to say things carefully, lest he consider me a challenge to his authority. As we started talking, he looked at me a bit more frequently, but when I put the investigation file on his desk, it was clear I had captured his full attention. Virtually by the second, I could see him starting to trust me, as he studied the document more and more thoroughly. Simmons later branded our report the best he'd ever seen and a model for subsequent reports by his own police department. Near the end of our meeting, he walked me over to a cork bulletin board where, under a bunch of papers, he had a bumper sticker that read, "Abuse an Animal, Go to Jail!" It was a memento, presented to Simmons by the Animal Legal Defense Fund, following a successful prosecution for felony animal cruelty, which is a tough case to make—in any jurisdiction. I knew then, for sure, that I was in the right office. The day's meetings ended with handshakes and Hale saying, "See you next week." I flew home.

Four days later, I left my home near Washington, DC, and made the eleven-plus hour drive to begin Operation Unbridled Spirit.

In the passenger seat was my right hand on rescues, Karla Goodson, ARC's director of outreach. Karla, who has since departed our organization to start her own business, was a founding member of ARC. When we began working together, Karla had many qualities that I look for when placing someone in a trusted position. She was motivated by our cause. She shared my philosophies. And she was open to learning about animal rescue from my perspective. I am certainly not a dictator, but I have been rescuing animals long enough that I have a pretty good idea of what works.

Although the raid is to be in Kentucky, we make our base of operations and construct our emergency shelter in a warehouse in Lebanon, Tennessee, about thirty miles outside of Nashville. The location is purely practical. The temporary space comes courtesy of a donor, and it puts us close to the resources of ARC's logistics coordinator, Amy Haverstick, a stalwart partner in our rescue missions. Amy came to ARC through a relationship we had with an organization she led. Amy repeatedly demonstrated her value and commitment. She is also one of the most genuine people you will ever meet. Amy is one of the first people we call when we deploy our emergency team. She has built relationships at a number of properties we have turned into emergency shelters. When you ask Amy to do a job, you know she will find the way, figure it out, and get it done.

Our emergency shelter is in the headquarters of an amusement park ride company. A beige building sided with corrugated metal, its lot is strewn with trucks and tractor-trailers of a wide range of ages and road-worthiness. Out back, sitting on the ground, is a neon-decorated billboard featuring a pinup cowgirl that says "Bar-B-Cutie: Lebanon's Finest Bar-B-Que Since 1948." The warehouse's interior has two main spaces, one about the size of a three-story basketball court, the other a bit larger but strewn with vestiges of county fairs and carnivals. There's a merry-go-round off in one corner, which sits near a pint-sized locomotive and train cars built to ferry kids around a carnival. The cars of a space shuttle ride are on a trailer across the room. There's a small kitchen to one side and some small rooms we will use as storage space and a makeshift veterinary office.

Setting up the space to function as our emergency shelter first requires a good cleaning and then some organization. We keep many of our supplies for deployments in a warehouse near Nashville, and after they are delivered, the warehouse becomes a hive of activity, as volunteers shuttle in supplies and set up fenced exercise areas and hundreds of dog pens. The larger of the two warehouse spaces gets cages destined for small dogs. They are stacked two high, in seven meticulously aligned rows of ten. The second space is filled with larger pens for larger dogs. The cages and pens outnumber the quantity of dogs we expect to rescue, almost all of whom we believe to be smaller dogs. We set up extras because we never know if estimates are correct. But in this case, there is another reason. Most who are setting up the areas are unaware that there may be a second raid in the near future. Even among our most loyal volunteers, it's just too risky to talk about possibilities that may not pan out.

Over the next day, more supplies—puppy pads, food, medication, shampoos, and grooming needs—are stacked and arranged. Normally, I am in the mix of every aspect of a deployment. This one, however, is unique. I spend the morning of the day before the raid having entirely unwelcome but urgent root canal surgery.

Wednesday evening, I gather our team into a small convoy, and we depart for Kentucky and the opportunity for at most a few hours of sleep.

Thursday, before sunrise, the team gathers in the hotel lobby. Everyone is outfitted in ARC dark battle dress uniform, or BDU: pants and blue t-shirts that have ARC's winged logo over the left breast and across the back. My vehicle takes the lead, followed by a couple of volunteers in their sport utility vehicles, a U-Haul truck full of portable kennels, a pickup truck pulling a trailer, a van from a partner organization that has a specialized cargo area for transporting animals, and a converted recreational vehicle called "The Spay Station." Featuring large images on its sides of happy dogs and cats, this RV not only has built-in crates, it is a climate-controlled operating room on wheels.

On the drive, I am even more on edge than usual. We carefully planned every detail of this raid, but since last night, I haven't been able to reach William Hale. Has something come up? Is there some other emergency? Have they changed their minds? Finally, he calls, assuring me that all is well. "That's a fucking relief," I yell to anyone paying attention behind me. After that, my mood considerably lightened, I pop in a CD and lead a sing-a-long to a recording by the late bluesman R. L. Burnside, with the refrain "That lazy motherfucker stole my check." We follow with a rousing version of Johnny Cash's "Folsom Prison Blues."

Our caravan's destination is Hale's office, although I am there for only a few minutes. The crew in my bus breaks off and heads for the Wayne County Courthouse, where we crowd into a small room with Sheriff Charles Boston and members of his department. On the surface, Boston, who will be with us all day long, would appear to be the rural sheriff from central casting. Gray haired and in his late sixties, with a moustache, pot belly, and prominent drawl, he is in a beige and brown uniform with a very shiny badge. Folksy as he may seem, Boston has prospered in a difficult niche. Sheriffs are elected officials, and Boston has been in his position since 2006. In election after election, Wayne County has voted overwhelmingly Republican, by as much as 75 percent. Boston is a Democrat.

On the wall in the courthouse is a framed certificate headlined "A Kentuckian Never Runs." It contains details about the state's stand-your-ground law.

We go over the official paperwork with Boston. Alicia looks over the documents and gives her verdict: "Looks great." With that, we are on the road to the property, only this time, people with guns, badges, and a warrant are in the lead.

In the owner's driveway, the theme of the moment is hurry up and wait. Until law enforcement gives the go-ahead, we are merely a group of bystanders. But when we get the high sign, things get busy in a hurry.

Job number one is assessing the property and the animals. We may have a recent, thorough report and all the authorities necessary to seize animals, but we need to rapidly get a grip on precisely what obstacles we face today. Joining me in that task is Dr. Robertson, our veterinarian, along with Karla and Alicia. Dr. Robertson will take a quick pass by the animals and judge, as best she can visually, if there are any dire health problems.

While Dr. Robertson is doing her job, Karla places a square of white plastic tape outside each area that contains animals, and she labels each one with a letter of the alphabet. Every animal will get a letter and a number, letting us know where that animal came from and when, in the sequence of rescues, we pulled her out. On this property, the tape labels go from A to LL. There are chain-link fenced dog runs, sheds, coops, kennels, hutches, and boxes full of dogs—clearly more than the seventy or so we expected. There are more inside the house. The day is getting warm and humid, and I know our work will last at least as long as the daylight. With a quick phone call, I get the rest of our caravan rolling. We can't afford to waste a minute.

As we finish assessing and tagging, our other vehicles arrive and about two dozen volunteers begin the day's manual labor. They put up a pair of canopy tents in the driveway, where the intake and medical teams will work. Volunteers put together dozens of portable cages. As this rescue operation is actually starting to look like a rescue operation, I assemble the entire team for a final briefing. "We've got a pretty horrific case inside," I tell them. "We've got approximately eighty dogs we'll be removing from this property. Some of them are in bad condition. It doesn't look like we've got anybody critical, but you're going to see some pretty ugly stuff today."

At this point, we know that one part of the operation we planned for is off the table: the miniature horses. The law in this state does not protect horses in the same way it protects dogs. Horses are considered agriculture, and there are exemptions for horses from certain anti-cruelty codes. These horses are not in sufficiently deteriorated conditions for us to make a successful case for their seizure.

As the briefing concludes, I remind the team about safety. It's going to be muddy and slippery. There will be feces virtually everywhere they step. I remind them about staying hydrated. I remind them that cellphone photographs and videos, Facebook posts, and tweets are off limits. The animals are evidence. Our still photographer, Amiee Stubbs, and our videographer, Brian Wilson, are the only ones authorized to make images. No information can be shared, even among friends or family, until the District Attorney authorizes us to publish it.

We operate under a command chart, which is posted on a white, dry-erase board. I will, of course, run the animal rescue side of the operation, in consultation, as necessary, with the sheriff and his staff, who are ultimately in charge. Next is the safety officer, who is one of our Tennessee volunteers and a nurse. She has the authority to shut down anything at any time, for safety purposes. I will also lead the extraction team. I will handle every animal first. In the few seconds available, I will assess the dog's physical condition, gauge her temperament, and then hand that animal over to a handler. Alicia will be on my team, as will my friend and co-author of this book, Rich Folkers, and Dan Stubbs, the husband of Amiee. A soft-spoken, easy-going guy, Dan is a former professional wrestler, as is Amiee. Rich is a longtime Washington photographer and writer, and my close friend for a decade. Karla will oversee intake. Handlers will stop at a table where Dr. Robertson will give each animal a cursory veterinary examination. Two notetakers will write down everything she says about the animal's condition, mindful that each word is potentially admissible in court. At a second table, dogs will be photographed: front, back, left, right, and top. Then each dog will go to one last team, which will pair her with her paperwork, put a tag around her neck with the letter code for the area from which she came and her number in the sequence of animals removed, and put her in a crate for transport.

Before we go in, I meet with the handlers to go over our techniques. I will extract each dog and, in most cases, put the dog on a plastic-encased wire leash. I will hold the dog in my right arm, tucked into my right hip, with the leash extended in my left hand so that, if he turns to bite, I can make the leash taut and pull his head away from me. Any dog, no matter how seemingly docile, can react to a stressful situation such as this—or we might accidentally touch a sore spot or injury on the animal that could cause him to react. During the handoff, we transfer the control quickly from one person to the other. It's a choreographed move in which I face the handler, who puts a fabric leash on the dog and removes mine. The handler then will turn away from me, holding the leash with her left hand, as I transfer the dog from my control. I only release completely when the recipient acknowledges control. In addition to the handlers for dogs we have also established a smaller group of experienced cat handlers who can step in when needed. We worry about these moves out of safety—for people and animals. Certainly we want to make sure no one is bitten or scratched. Control of the animal is paramount. When two people are attempting to handle a rescued dog or cat equally, there really is no control. The last thing I am willing to do is accidentally lose a dog or cat we just saved from a life of hell.

I remind the handlers that they will be breathing some toxic air. Well-filtered masks are a necessity. Because I will be exposed to the most ammonia, I wear a commercial-grade respirator with removable canisters. The longer you'll be in fouled air, the heavier a mask I want you to wear.

The instructions over, the last questions answered, I have one last marching order for the rescue team: "Let's go fulfill our promise of new life."

We know from our assessment just an hour ago that one dog is running free in the backyard. It's only logical that we remove her first, in what will also be the day's first test of our systems and protocols. This dog is a special case. The puppy mill owner warned a member of our team that this dog is not hers, that she may be unpredictable. "She's a rescue," the puppy mill owner said. The fearsome dog is a Yorkie, and she appears to tip the scales at about five pounds. She's not a particularly difficult catch. The little girl looks pitifully neglected. She trembles mightily, but she doesn't try to bite me or escape.

In a textbook maneuver, I hand her to Alicia, who heads gingerly but quickly toward the intake tents. Dr. Robertson jumps into action with the medical evaluation, which shows the tiny dog is missing all of her teeth, except for the upper canines. She has fleas. Hair loss is severe; patches of skin are visible where her coat should be. She has enlarged lymph nodes, a heart murmur, and a mass on one of her rear legs. The first dog of a rescue is always notable, but there is not much time to dwell on the bigger picture, to see this dog as a metaphor. We all know this is but the first dog whose suffering will end today. Soon enough, they will all be rescues.

During the course of the morning, the puppy mill's owner is not allowed into her house. A Wayne County detective, Bryan Worley, stays with her. For the most part, she sits in the shade smoking, drinking Cokes, and occasionally shooting cellphone photographs of the rescue team. She alternates between the middle of the yard and the steps of a camper trailer at the far side of the property from where we are working. At one point, she can be heard asking Worley, "Why would I neglect dogs?" She agrees to come into the backyard, to unlock one small outbuilding. On the way, she stops at one dog hutch and leans over to kiss a dog through the cage wires, saying, in a deep, raspy voice, "Hey, baby." She addresses the one large dog on the property more sharply. "Sit," she yells. "I said sit now!" At times, the property owner puts her head in her hands and breaks into loud, wailing sobs. Midway through the morning, she becomes particularly agitated and complains she is in medical distress. The authorities call an ambulance. Emergency medical technicians check her out and leave.

With access to everything we need, with our roles defined and our routine tested, it's time to get methodical.

The most prominent feature of the backyard is a round, above-ground swimming pool. Everywhere else there are dogs. These are smaller breeds: Pomeranians, Maltese, Yorkies, Shih Tzus, French bulldogs, Pekingese, and Chihuahuas, plus some others less easy to peg. A few, particularly the French bulldogs, are in kennels where they can stand and turn around, but not much more. Some have rough-hewn, plywood houses with doors that have been enlarged by some combination of rot and teeth. Clean water and fresh food are in short supply.

Conditions go downhill as the size of the dogs we find decreases. Some of them are in structures more akin to a rabbit hutch than a dog kennel. They are made from unfinished two-by-four lumber, their walls and floors made of wire. There are no actual floors. Walk past, and one pair of eyes appears. Then another. Then four or five more. Some dogs live in enclosures with chicken wire bottoms. Their feet can't slip through the floor only because dried feces have stuck, accumulated, and created a surface of sorts to stand on. The floors of other enclosures—with easily a dozen dogs inside each one—are made of wire spaced two to three inches apart. The dogs in those pens have become adept at walking along the few boards to which the wire is attached—or balancing, circus-like on the wires—on paws marked by cracked, overgrown nails that look as if they would make walking on the ground impossible. The longhaired breeds have fur that is matted to their skin, with accumulated feces holding their coats down into a disgusting mass of mats. Accumulated discharge from their eyes stains many muzzles. Many have splotches of fur missing, their skin red and irritated. Just a glance at the underside of most reveals colonies of fleas moving like a lengthy traffic back-up at rush hour.

After the first dozen or so dogs are out, the line at the intake table is growing long, and I realize it's time to take a break. Rescues tend to move faster the longer they go on. Teams become synchronized, and things just start to click. The first batch of dogs we found consisted mainly of adult dogs. As we proceed, there are more pregnant dogs and mothers with pups. Pulling them out, I am utterly aware that dogs don't understand conversation. But as any animal lover knows, they understand tone. I try to talk to each one before I pull her from an enclosure. "Hi, my love, can I come in and see you?" "Hi, my love. Your suffering ends now."

One enclosure, which had been noted in our undercover investigators' report, is about five feet tall and sits on sloping ground, its wooden legs resting precariously on cinderblocks. There appears to be just one dog inside, but as I remove her, I notice a box about the size of a window air conditioner on the side. Craning my neck in, I catch sight of a puppy. There are actually three. They have nothing to lie on except a filthy piece of feces-encrusted blanket. Their eyes are not yet fully open; they are not more than ten days old. I reach around in the box, making sure I can feel no more puppies. Thinking I have them all isn't enough, though. To be sure it's empty, I ask Dan to rip the box apart, which is something I will ask him to do several more times during the day.

Mothers and puppies go to the front of the medical line, especially brachycephalic breeds like French bulldogs and Pekingese, with flat and wide skull shapes who have breathing issues, especially in hot weather. One of the French bulldog mothers is in distress and requires intravenous fluids.

When clearing out a place like this, I almost always find one outbuilding that is the sickening heart of a puppy mill. These are often ramshackle, barn-shaped buildings the size of a large garden shed. When I open the door to this outbuilding today, the escaping heat and ammonia odor are overpowering, to the point that my eyes well up immediately. I order everyone else out. With my mask secure and my eyes adjusting to the dark space, I see two parallel rows of what appear to be white, built-in benches, five per side. They are actually boxes made of rusted, flimsy metal over light, foam cores. With the lids closed, there is no circulating air and certainly no light. As I open each lid, heads pop out—Chihuahuas, Yorkies, Pugs. These boxes are where mothers are tossed, to give birth and nurse. The boxes have rubber doggie doors that lead out to some of the above-ground pens with wide-spaced wire floors, where the mother dogs, whose feet may have never touched the ground, join the circus balancing act. Their eyes are vacant. Like others, their nails are so long they are curling back toward the pads of their feet. Most handlers come just to the door of the outbuilding, where I meet them with dogs. I ask our traditional tight space handler Kayce Hackett to crawl into the outside pens, to nudge dogs toward me. This part of the drill is so familiar that I only need glance at Kayce, and she jumps in. Our pace is the quickest of the day. The dogs want to escape this hell, and so do we.

We save the inside of the house for last. The dogs are in shade and the air is at least marginally better. I know they are contained, so I figure the others are the priority to remove first. The house also proves an unexpected crescendo to the day. The front door opens to the living room, which is barely passable. Its floors are coated with feces, and nearly every inch of space is occupied by something. In one corner is what passes for office space; in another, a pile to the ceiling of religious memorabilia. Furniture is covered with dirty throws. Almost the only light in the room is the glow of an old, small, cathode-ray TV monitor connected to a security camera watching the street. I had assessed the house in the morning and, making a quick pass in the afternoon, I notice several dogs aren't there, in particular a Maltese and three pups. I pride myself on being thorough, and you won't ever see our team leaving behind any animals we can lawfully rescue. I call in the sheriff, who is emphatic that neither the owner nor her husband or anyone could have snuck in to squirrel away or remove dogs. Still, I send two teams of volunteers to search the house while I continue removing dogs we know are there.

The owner had, by this time, been arrested. Contacted by the sheriff, she volunteered that one dog was in the basement. We quickly find that one, but not the others. The second two-man volunteer team moves through the upper floor of the house, with a flashlight-toting Dan taking the lead and Rich at his side. They look over, under, and inside—including the refrigerator, microwave, kitchen cabinets, and the rest of the filthy kitchen. They look under blankets and behind throw pillows. They look in one bedroom, which is eerily stacked with figurines, busts, and cartoonish carved dolls that would unnerve anyone who finds clowns creepy. Another bedroom is passable only for the first two feet or so; the windows are covered with spider webs so old they are three-dimensional. A back bedroom, the master, has a light on, its ceiling fan still running, and a clock radio playing a country station. The bed is coated with dog feces. At the back of the room is a walk-in closet crammed with clothing and assorted junk. Every room reeks of stale cigarette smoke. But no dogs. Dan and Rich make a final pass. Still nothing.

As they are about to leave, grudgingly acknowledging the futility of the moment, they notice, in the back of the walk-in closet, a doorknob almost completely obscured by a hanging storage rack. Not knowing what might be behind that door—it could be a person—they open it just a crack. As Dan's flashlight casts a narrow beam to the ceiling and down to the floor, they catch sight of a tiny, white body and a pair of eyes reflecting the light. It's the Maltese.

Moments later, while I'm in the front yard, talking with my team about next steps, Dan bursts out the door and yells, "We found them!" I bolt inside, grab the mother and the three pups, hand them to Dan and Rich, and follow them outside. It is the day's high point, one of those moments you remember because of its improbability and also the grace note it brings to a day of cruelty confronted. The Maltese mother is the day's last rescue. She is dog number one hundred twenty two.

As soon as they are full, vehicles from our convoy head back to Tennessee and the emergency shelter. How the case will be adjudicated and how custody of the animals will be resolved is, at this point, anything but certain. Kentucky does not have any law requiring a custody hearing for dogs seized in a cruelty case. We learn that the puppy mill owner, who has now bonded out of jail, is refusing to sign over the dogs, cats, and birds we have removed from the property. If she takes a hard line, I could be forced to care for them, as evidence, until her criminal trial is adjudicated, perhaps for as long as a year or even two. Bryan Worley, the detective, grabs me, and we head off to meet the owner at a relative's house, in the hope we can talk her into surrender. Our efforts are unsuccessful. She wants to negotiate. She wants to keep twenty dogs. When I balk, she asks me for a number. I tell her it's zero. "If you want to go this direction, I will care for every one of these dogs until we go to trial. And then I will seek reimbursement for every penny I spent on their care." Over the next few days she leaves half a dozen messages on my cellphone voicemail. I ignore them all.

Ultimately she relents. The animals belong to ARC.

With all of the dogs on the way to the shelter after the raid, we have tents to break down, trash to pick up, and vehicles to repack. Mine is the last to leave, partly because a TV crew has arrived on the scene, asking to interview me. Finally, with law enforcement thanked and everything packed, the rescue is over. Alicia takes the wheel. When we are no more than a handful of miles down the road, heading up a long, uphill stretch of two-lane road, she calls to the back: "I'm not getting any power." One look at the dashboard shows the problem: The temperature gauge is off the charts. A dozen or so bottles of water poured into the empty radiator reservoir don't fill it. We can see steam coming from the undercarriage. We coast downhill, in the direction of what our GPS tells us should be a gas station. There is no gas station. After giving the engine time to cool, we decide to shoot for a Walmart store just a few miles away. We don't make it. As a harvest moon begins to rise above the horizon, we come to a stop at the entrance of a high school. Our other vehicles are now hours away. I have five exhausted, hungry people who smell very literally like crap, and we are stuck.

I can think of only one option. I call the Wayne County Sheriff's Office and convince the night person to relay a message to Bryan Worley. In a surprisingly few minutes, he pulls up behind our dead vehicle in an unmarked car, with lights flashing. He is wearing shorts and an Army t-shirt. We interrupted his workout. I jump in his car, and minutes later we return, with me behind the wheel of an almost new sheriff's van. Not just any van, mind you. This is the kind they use to transport prisoners, with a Plexiglas partition behind the front seats. And off we go, five of us heading for Tennessee in a prominently marked law enforcement vehicle. I have two more television crews waiting for me when we return, so there's no time to waste. Fortunately, on this night, we are not likely to be pulled over.

It is several hours after dark when we finally pull in to the emergency shelter. When we get close, I turn to the others in the van and say what we all have noticed: "It smells like a puppy mill in here."

CHAPTER TWO

PURSUING COMPASSION

The morning after the raid, our emergency shelter is no longer a warehouse in waiting. The seventy cages that were neatly stacked and prepped for occupancy are now full of four-legged residents. Several dozen more cages have been moved into the area, and they are all full, too. The section for expectant and new mothers is lined with litters of puppies busily nursing. Volunteers move through the aisles in waves, cleaning crates, offering food, and refilling water bowls. Aside from medical exams or treatment, the dogs can be held only briefly by gloves-wearing team members while their crates are being cleaned. Most of the dogs are still crusted with dried mud, urine, and feces. During the next two days, veterinarians will give each dog a thorough examination, after which volunteer groomers will work their magic. Most of the longhaired breeds will require buzz cuts. All of the dogs will have their nails trimmed, followed by a bath and blow dry. But in a reminder of the case that brought us here, the groomers will place in plastic bags the filthy, matted fur and grotesquely overgrown nails they remove from each dog. For now, the contents of the bags are evidence.

This sea of dogs is an impressive sight, and it is impossible to look at them without thinking of the unconscionable conditions that were their entire existence less than twenty-four hours ago. Some of the dogs bark excitedly and attempt to approach people walking by. Others are more taciturn and quiet. The Maltese mother is with three puppies whom we are not certain are actually hers. But she struggles mightily, with an air of quiet dignity, to care for them. For all of the dogs, their journey from victim to treasured companion has just begun—literally and figuratively.

When people see one of our operations in action or when I show them photographs and video of the nightmarish puppy mill raid we just led, even the most ardent animal lovers often ask why I would choose, again and again, to walk into such horrible, cruel, dispiriting places. Underlying the question is, I suppose, a feeling that I am trying to fix an unfixable problem. But one thing I am not is an unrealistic dreamer. I have worked in the animal protection field for all of my career: in humane law enforcement, animal sheltering, and large-scale animal rescue. I have rescued tens of thousands of animals after natural disasters and in barbaric places of human-devised suffering.

I am resolved to see a day, in my lifetime, when no more puppy mills remain. When that domino falls, I believe we can end all factory production of animals. There are, by my best estimate, between 10,000 and 15,000 puppy mills in the United States alone, but there is just one Animal Rescue Corps. I am not here, in a warehouse in Tennessee, surrounded by innocent victims of humans, to chase an impossible dream. I am here because I know that every time my team and I deploy, we don't just save animals; we change attitudes. We inspire compassion. People are persuaded by seeing, in their communities, what we do for castaways and the victims of cruelty. Not only do we fix a single problem, we also inspire communities to seek justice, address issues of animal treatment, and demonstrate their concern by influencing change in laws and policy. Our cause is spreading, and it will continue to spread and persuade, leading to new thinking and new legislation, because of the transformative power of compassion.

Compassion is not the same as sympathy. Sympathy is largely about commiseration, about pure, undiluted emotion. When we witness a child in loathsome conditions, when we look into the mournful eyes of an abandoned or abused puppy, it's natural to feel an ache, to yearn to offer love and affection, to have the parental desire to make it all better, even when we may not know how. Sympathy is about feeling the sorrows of others. The people who volunteer with ARC are amazingly committed, selfless individuals. They have big hearts; they feel deeply for the animals our society casts off or those who live in abuse and neglect. Big-hearted people like them look for some way to channel their sympathy. They seek some way, any way, to help. They have a mix of sympathy and passion that drives them to volunteer or donate. It is my obligation to respect their feelings, to thank them for their commitment, and to channel their passion and sympathy in practical ways. The volunteers in our emergency shelter are the embodiment of what sympathetic, caring people can do. When the time comes that they are able to pull dogs close and hug them—when the evidence is collected, the medical exams are complete, and the dogs are bathed and groomed—more than a few volunteers (most, if not all of them, actually) will shed some well-earned tears.

My involvement must be different. I must be driven by my professionalism as much as I am by my heart, propelled by knowledge, study, and intense preparation. When I walk through an emergency shelter, you will see me checking in with each of the animals, ensuring they are happy with their temporary accommodations, talking to them, rubbing a nose or offering a gentle pat, and, yes, even shedding a tear or two. But I must be mindful not to celebrate at a time when much work remains. I care deeply about the animals entrusted to my care. I care deeply about the people who look after them. I strive to understand all of their emotions. Their sympathy and empathy inspire me to understand, comprehend, study, lead, and continually improve. I must do all I can to provide the best possible outcomes, and I must also be prepared for the worst. I must consider the practical along with the potential, the legal along with the ethical, the hearts that are already open, and the confrontations to come with those whose hearts are closed and abusive. I have come to realize that one of my tasks is managing and channeling the sympathies of extraordinarily dedicated people. I see compassion as sympathy and empathy driven by conviction and professionalism.

I have come to this place, to this rescue, to this emergency shelter because of a life I devote to compassion, to ending suffering and striving to create the world I wish to see, driven by a deeply held conviction of the things animals are not. Animals are not property. They are not simply pets, put here for human enjoyment. Animals are not possessions or livestock. To me, they are not food. Animals are not crude beasts, solely driven by reflex or instinct. Animals are not toys or accessories. Animals are not things or an "it."

Animals live and breathe; they think, feel, and have emotions and moods. They make choices. And I believe they have a voice. I realize, of course, that animals do not utter words. They do not have what science would describe as a language. Yet animals do speak to us. Their "language" has many more components than a bark, tail wag, or growl. Animals communicate among themselves and to us in myriad ways—if we do the hard work of learning their subtleties. Animals speak through their bodies, in the way they hold their heads, and by holding or averting eye contact. They tell us when they are happy, sad, or fearful, and when our attention is wanted or unwanted. They tell us when we are forcing ourselves on them. They speak through their tails, scales, noses, and trunks. If animals were able to speak in words, I believe they would tell us to stop taking them from their habitats, stop caging them, stop chaining them, and stop abusing, torturing, killing, and exploiting them.

These pages are an opportunity for me to tell you about my life rescuing animals, about missions to save animals in conditions beyond comfortable description. This book is also a chance to explain the world I see and how, together, I firmly believe we can create it.

There is a nine-word quote most often attributed to Mahatma Gandhi that guides my life: "Be the change you wish to see in the world." Gandhi also said, "The greatness of a nation and its moral progress can be judged by the way its animals are treated." I believe that animals have rights. I respect all life. My conviction is that people, if they listen to animals, will give them greater voice and protect them.

We demonstrate conviction by our actions. I believe we also show our commitment to change by the words we choose. In the still-unfinished work of the American civil rights movement, we have learned that words can sting, that certain terms are vile and inappropriate. In the greater awareness of people with intellectual and developmental disabilities, a hateful word is moving toward extinction. Enlightened Americans accept that people whom society has belittled deserve respect. Advocates on their behalf work to change our discourse. They work to change our society—and individual hearts and minds. We are still learning how to respect women and, as a society, how better to accept people of all genders and sexual orientations. Language is not simply political correctness taking over. It is a sign of a compassionate and equitable future.

Compassion for animals means we must consider how we refer to them. An animal in my care is a "he" or a "she," not an "it." Despite what antiquated laws may say, I do not refer to animals as property. They are not to be owned. We are their companions and their guardians. We demonstrate our conviction, our concern, our respect for others in ways simple and complex. Words matter—about people and animals. Compassion demands respect. And the hard work continues.

The rescue phase of Operation Unbridled Spirit is just hours old, yet members of our team at the emergency shelter are aware that something else is up. There is, after all, that entire second section of the warehouse filled with large cages and pens. People know there must be a second rescue afoot, but few know where, or that it will be today. It's a lot to ask a group of people, many of whom have not had more than three hours of sleep. Yet no one complains.

Our destination is Mississippi, a small town not far from Tupelo, about five hours away. Our caravan is smaller than the previous day's group. We believe we are going after just a few dozen or so larger breed dogs. We have not had an undercover operative on this property, nor do we have a report in hand. Local authorities contacted ARC and asked us to come in, so precisely what we will find is something of a question.

As we arrive at the sheriff's office in Union County, the sky is turning dark. A rainstorm is approaching. We head to a staging area. Dr. Robertson and I get into the sheriff's pickup truck for a quick assessment of the property, leaving Karla, Alicia, Rich, and Amiee behind. They send word to the rest of our vehicles to get rolling toward the gravel staging area. It's already the afternoon, and wet weather will make this a slow operation. We need to be ready to roll.

We come back almost an hour later. Stepping into the now-steady rain, it is obvious to everyone that Dr. Robertson is struggling mightily to keep her emotions in check. I try to hide the fact that I am on edge, too.

We head inside the Spay Station, to speak confidentially with the local officials. I ask Alicia to join us, to get a legal perspective. What we have found are conditions that, while unacceptable in my view, are not sufficiently negligent or abusive for us to make a case that animals must be seized. Based on what we have seen, Alicia is not able to find any legal grounds that justify a seizure. The final call falls to the sheriff, but we all know what the outcome is going to be.

Coming this far in the belief we can save more lives, and then coming up empty, is an unhappy outcome. It isn't the way I like to operate. But there is more to the story. In the house we just visited, there are three children living in conditions I find difficult to accept. They are home-schooled and, according to a schedule posted on the refrigerator, they are the family work force and the full-time operators of this animal breeding operation. They spend many hours each day taking care of animals, both dogs and horses. They are not allowed off the property. They have jobs and home school, and punishments if their parents judge that they have failed at either. The children have no time or opportunity to relax or play, nor are they allowed to socialize with others. It is a situation neither Dr. Robertson nor I have faced before, and we react not as dispatched professionals but as compassionate people, as sympathetic people, as parents. We pledge any effort we can offer, including advising the sheriff on even small potential animal violations he can use to get back on the property to check on the children. But for the most part, we have nothing to offer. In my life, one of the worst feelings—and one of the rarest—is to be powerless.

When it is clear no animal rescue will happen, the sheriff steps out into the storm, shakes the hand of every member of my team, apologizes for inconveniencing us, and leaves. On the drive back to Tennessee, the rain picks up until the lane markers on the interstate are barely visible, with downpours beating loudly on the roof of the van. I spend some time thinking about my daughters, my son, and about the very notion of compassion, which I have once again been reminded can't know boundaries.

The question remains, though: Is compassion enough? To eliminate suffering, to change how we regard animals, to change how we regard children, requires societal change. It requires new laws. It requires trained and responsive law enforcement. It requires awareness by consumers. It requires more than ARC and other organizations taking direct action. Yet I believe what we do is greater than each place we change, each community we affect. We raid puppy mills and other hellholes that profit from animal suffering, one horrible place at a time, but we also influence people in those communities, and they, in turn, make more responsible decisions in their lives. They become our agents of change. What I do prompts people to listen to my message—not an overbearing animal rights or human rights agenda, but a compassionate message about respect and valuing all life and addressing injustice.

Doing that—one animal, one industry, one community, one state at a time—takes stamina, patience, money, and determination, but I believe it is the way to change our country and beyond. That snowball is rolling downhill. It is picking up speed, and it will grow ever larger. I believe I will live to see some of the changes I seek, and I am determined that our work will be a catalyst for a truly humane society.

As Operation Unbridled Spirit progresses from rescue to a sheltering operation, we are able to focus more on assessment and enrichment, preparing animals for futures in permanent, loving homes. In the days ahead, placement partners from non-profit shelters, rescue groups, and foster networks throughout North America will move animals from our shelter to valued lives. It is the most gratifying stage of our work.

On Sunday morning, as I walk through the hotel lobby, about to head for the emergency shelter, a woman of grandmotherly age, wearing a coral-colored jogging suit, rises from her table at the breakfast bar and walks over to me. "Are y'all the people that went into that place in Kentucky?" she asks. "I'm just so impressed and so proud of you."

One at a time.

CHAPTER THREE

PUNK AND PROUD

As much as I am uncomfortable with the notion, people sometimes call me a hero, which I realize is simply an extension of the sympathy they feel for the animals my colleagues and I rescue. People who have embraced their compassion for animals see pictures of ARC removing sick, matted, mistreated animals from horrific places; they see me on video in the middle of a rescue, and often their first thought is, *I could never do that. I couldn't stand seeing all those sad eyes. It would just be too emotional.* And so those people elevate me. They assume I must be special because I do what they don't believe they could. But I make no claim to heroism. My work and my mission drive me. My goal, to which I dedicate my life, is ending as much suffering as I can, leaving a legacy of compassion.

I am often approached in the days after a puppy mill rescue operation by people who thank me for looking after innocent creatures. A moment like that is a challenge, a balancing act. I want that person to feel good about our meeting. I want to plant in that person a seed that will further our collective efforts to end suffering. So I give them what they are looking for. When someone recognizes me, I always stop. I always give him at least a few moments of my undivided attention, and I try to conclude the conversation with the feeling—a sincere feeling—that we can all make a difference in the world.

The path to a life of compassion is different for each of us. For some, it is a lifetime commitment, passed from generation to generation. For others, compassion comes from a collection of life experiences that make a mark. My path was a unique one, borne from an early life none of us would likely choose. But it was also an early life that made me who I am today. I am relating that story here as a reminder that we are all unique, that our stories may not have idyllic beginnings, but that the power of compassion is transcendent.

I was born February 24, 1968, in Los Angeles County, California. I was the middle child, with one sister five years older and one a year younger. My parents divorced when I was about six years old. I went to live with my father in Orange County. We weren't poor, but neither were we, by any means, well off. My father went to work, and I mostly had to fend for myself. I returned home from school each day and waited for my father to call and check in. Some days that call didn't come, and I became bolder as time went on, setting my own schedule. I was a pretty solitary kid with few friends. It wasn't uncommon for me to find nothing in the refrigerator at home, so part of my routine became a stop at a convenience store, where I would stuff a package of hot dogs down the front of my pants and a Captain America comic book in the back.

Purloined Captain America comics allowed me to exercise a vivid imagination, and they also provided me my first hero. Captain America defeated the Nazis. He was America's hero. The character is still a favorite of mine and is the source of one of my favorite quotes: "I believe in an idea, an idea that a single individual who has the right heart and the right mind that is consumed with a single purpose, that one man can win a war. Give that one man a group of soldiers with the same conviction, and you can change the world."

Not long after I moved in with my father, we visited the home of one of his friends. My father was inside talking to the adults, and I was in the backyard with the kid of the house, who was about my age. He had a BB gun. I had never had a toy like that. In fact, I had never had many toys. But my grandfather had a BB gun. He was a fascinating figure. He had lived for a time as a hobo, riding the rails, and had spent a little time "in the pokey" for petty offenses. And he painted—a passion I am most grateful to have inherited from him. When we visited my grandfather in his trailer, I recall the excitement of going out back and shooting at beer cans. It was an honor to shoot that gun—a feeling of responsibility coupled with an air of power. But I was always supervised.

This kid in the backyard not only had a BB gun, but he shot it without any parental supervision. I was amazed at how much responsibility he had—being allowed to handle that gun all by himself meant he was trusted beyond his years. In hindsight, I realize that he was just an unsupervised kid with an unsafe toy. But in that moment, his gun was power. It was prestige.

We took turns handling the gun and aiming it at all kinds of objects, shooting at a few. One of them was a sparrow I spied in a nearby magnolia tree, maybe eight feet from me, sitting on a branch in the shade. I aimed at the sparrow. He was square in the gun sight.

"Go ahead and pull the trigger," the boy said.

"Really? I can do this? I'm allowed?"

He said yes.

I felt even more powerful. Suddenly I was a hunter. I looked down the barrel of the BB rifle. I checked again to make sure the bird was aligned in the gun's crude sight. My aim was sure. And I pulled the trigger. It was a perfect shot.

The bird fell to the ground, flailing and bleeding, bouncing off several branches as he dropped.

The elapsed time from my shot until he hit the ground was at most a second or two. Yet in that tiny fraction of time, my power and my bravado melted. I went from control and power to sympathy and sorrow. And regret.

I let the gun fall, and I went to the bird. I dropped to my knees and put my hands around him, as if to protect him from further hurt.

"What do we do?" I asked.

"You've got to put him out of his misery," the boy said.

"What do you mean? How do I do that?"

"He's suffering. Now you have to kill him. Bottle cap," he said, with a gesture that made clear I should twist the bird's head like I would unscrew a bottle cap, to break his neck.

I picked up the dying bird as gingerly as I knew how. He was still flailing. I had blood all over my hands. I was trying not to hurt him, but I could tell that, simply by holding him, I was magnifying his pain. I needed to find a way to do what the boy told me. Finally he said, "Man, you just gotta do it. Grip him firm and twist his head like a bottle cap."

And I did.

I killed him.

The emotions hit me like a wave. *What have I done? Why did I make him suffer? Why did I kill him? I did not have the right to do this.*

That incident happened more than thirty-five years ago. But it remains a story as fresh as yesterday, and I can still summon the feeling in my stomach when I took that life. For a lot of kids, I suppose that moment would be a small one. For me, I will never forget it, even though I soon dismissed it at the time.

The one real break I had from my days of school and stealing was playing soccer. I was on a team through most of my elementary school years, as a goalie. I was pretty good and a member of a pretty good team. I loved the responsibility of guarding the net, of saving or losing the day. It was my first time in a leadership position and I appreciated it—to the extent any kid can process such a concept. Goalie is a good position for a headstrong, independent kid. I relished the role.

Our team won the southern California championship. We played the state championship at the Rose Bowl. I don't remember if we won, but as a result of that game, I was selected for an all-state championship team. They sent us north in California to San Jose, east to Kalamazoo, Michigan, and across the Atlantic to London.

It was about this time that the punk rock movement was an exploding cultural phenomenon in England. I got an up-close look at the punk scene from the window of a tour bus. Making our way through the streets of London, we drove past groups of tough-looking people with strange hair and provocative sneers. On one ride, I summoned my pre-teen courage and flashed a peace sign at one punk kid on the street below. He came right next to the bus, gave me the finger and spat on the window. In that momentary encounter, I was enamored. This person had no fear of anyone or anything. Everything about him said he rejected everything about most everyone else. He was free of all constraints. I pictured myself as him. I knew nothing then of the music that unified the punks or what their rebellion was about, but something I couldn't describe—and in some ways I still can't describe—took hold.

One of the few connections I had with my father was music. A rare pleasant memory I have is driving places with him, with the soft rock album "The Best of Bread" playing on his eight-track tape player. At that time, music was how I learned about so many things, not only in the lyrics but also in the covers of albums. I went to record stores and leafed through the shelves, lingering over punk rock music. The first album I took home was the eponymous debut album by the English band The Clash. I stole it. The three-chord songs, the tempo, and the beat all thrilled me, and the in-your-face glare of the band members on the cover was a look I wanted to emulate.

I became increasingly rebellious. Punk was what I wanted. At about the age of eleven, I began running away from home for short periods of time. Being on my own and possibly getting into trouble was more enticing than being alone at home. There were times I would go back home and other times when my father would look for me. How long I stayed home depended mostly on whether I was in school, where I certainly wasn't getting on the honor roll.

In the late seventies, the punk scene had made it in earnest from England to the U.S. and to my community. My route to school took me past a liquor store and an alley where a group of punks hung out. They intrigued me: the rebellion, the clothes, the "I don't have to take this shit from anyone" attitude. But I kept my distance. The punks were on the side of the street I needed to be on, but rather than walking through them I went around. Over time, though, my curiosity and bravado got the better of me and I began edging closer and closer. I wanted to test the waters. The closer I got, the more they would curse or throw things at me, including the occasional bottle. One day, for no better reason than not allowing someone else to choose my path, I decided to confront the punks and walk right past them.

There must have been three or four of them. One of the punks, a little jerk, swaggered up to me and blocked my way. One of the others told him to leave me alone, but he persisted, saying threatening things to me. I tried to go around. He moved again to block my way, but this time he went right for me, throwing me up against a wall. Again, one of the other punks told him to leave me alone, and this time he listened. I went on my way. But to me, this was now my side of the street. I had won the showdown because I refused to back down.

From that day on, the punks seemed to acknowledge my nerve, and they let me pass freely. Eventually, with more interaction and time hanging out, they realized I was a kid with problems—as, no doubt, they were, too. I grew closer and closer to them, and they eventually talked me into leaving home.

The punk movement, especially in its heyday, is frequently characterized as anarchic and violent, a group of misfits who conformed to a lifestyle of weird hair, leather, and spikes. That isn't the life I knew. Certainly there were violent punks, and we were aggressive, but to us, it was mostly a movement about change. Before punks were the flower children, the hippies. Their way of life was about opposition to the Vietnam War, sexual freedom, experimentation with drugs, and a counterculture.

Punks were distinct. As I lived it and studied it in the lyrics of its songs, the punk movement was about individuals thinking for themselves and questioning everything we had been told: history, authority, tradition. It was the first—and at that time—the only thing in which I ever believed.

I see those punk days as a historical movement, and I was on its front lines. We challenged values in just about every way. Punk was a badge of defiance. Of course, the look was important to us. Before there were punks, who had ever seen someone with a safety pin in his ear or a green Mohawk? Punk gave me a community in which I felt safe to express my anger. We were there for one another. It was the first real sense of family I had ever felt. Being just a kid, I didn't entirely understand the need for change punks believed in or comprehend all of the movement's politics, but I bought into them anyway. They made sense. What I learned was mostly about non-conformity, that I would make up my own mind. I would think for myself. Despite stereotypes and appearances, I saw—and still see—the influence of punks on my life as positive. Punk gave us an avenue to be ourselves, to define ourselves. All of the physical manifestations were the symbols of the moment; what defined us, though, was a punk mindset, expressed in hard-driving music.

Of course, my punk friends got me into everything. I drank and took drugs at an age when I should have been going to school and playing video games. Our goal was to wake up and get numb. As far as I knew, no one was looking for me. We panhandled for money, and then we resumed getting numb. And then there was music.

The first punk show I remember attending was in the L.A. area. There were a number of bands in the line-up, including one I still follow, Social Distortion. It was my first show of any kind, and I plunged right into the mosh pit—thrashing, as we called it, or slam dancing. In a circle in front of the stage, we would march and flail our arms in synch with the music. There was a rhythm to our dancing; it wasn't just chaos. It really was a sweet symphony of expressive aggression. The gestures seemed violent, but it felt productive, a group manifestation of feelings. The sweat, the stench, the random punches in the face or the body—blows that weren't directed at anyone but happened to connect—were an incredible feeling, a release from the confines of my life. I was expressing who I was and how I felt, feeling free. It was all about the energy, the beat, the tempo, the apparent chaos. I felt alive in a mosh pit. I didn't emerge until the show was over—bloody, sweaty, exhausted, and sober, because I had worked everything out of my system. I felt a sense of accomplishment.

When I first became a punk, I followed English bands like the Sex Pistols, The Clash, Stiff Little Fingers, and Generation X. As I got further into the punk scene, I learned there was a southern California genre that included Social Distortion, Fear, The Circle Jerks, Black Flag, T.S.O.L., The Germs, The Dead Kennedys, and Agent Orange. We went to every show we could. Of course, I had no money to pay for the shows, and there was always someone at the door using a rubber stamp to mark the back of your hand as proof of payment. Fortunately, I learned how to lick the back of my hand and hold it firmly against the hand of a paying customer to transfer a believable amount of the rubber stamp ink.

As I've said, being a punk meant thinking your own way. That wasn't always easy. I remember a young couple in our group. They had a young child. When they needed diapers or other baby supplies, they would send me into a store alone to get those items. They feared that a young punk rock couple with a baby would automatically spur a call to child protective services. Later, when I realized they were seriously neglecting the child, I made an anonymous call to the authorities. I tussled with myself over making the call, over trusting a segment of society that punks distrusted, but I decided not to turn my back on a suffering child.

At one point in my mid-teen years, I wound up back with my father for a short time. He didn't really want me there, though. We no longer had any kind of relationship, and neither of us expressed any desire to rekindle it, so he shipped me across the country to Annandale, Virginia, a suburb of Washington, DC, to live with my mother. I bounced in and out of her house for about a year.

As the punk movement continued to spread, it also diversified. There were street punks like me but also skinheads, straight edge punks, and numerous other gradations. Those worlds collided for me in D.C.

Members of the punk community developed reputations that traveled with them. I had obtained a certain notoriety in Los Angeles, in no small part because of how young I was, and that reputation quickly caught up with me in Washington. However, the D.C. area was heavily influenced—dominated, really—by a whole different kind of punk.

In 1981 a band called Minor Threat released a song called "Straight Edge," written by its leader, Ian MacKaye, who founded Dischord Records, a company that still exists today. With the refrain "I've got the straight edge," the song's lyrics amounted to an anthem for the punk sect it inspired, capped by the lines "I'm a person just like you/But I've got better things to do."

The straight edge punks didn't believe in drinking, drugging, or fighting. Suffice it to say the straight edge punks didn't like me and I didn't like them. They saw themselves as superior, as sensitive punks. They saw people like me as the bottom of the barrel. And I, in turn, chafed at being introduced to a sector of the punk world with rules. I wasn't ready for punk rock with limitations.

By the time I was fifteen years old, the streets were my only home. Living on the streets of D.C. at that time meant my community was much broader than just punks; it was a society of the homeless. My bed was a steam grate in front of a bank on Washington's famed Dupont Circle, an area where businesspeople in wool suits regularly stepped over homeless people. In that homeless community, you learned where to go at what time of the day, particularly to meet the soup trucks in different parts of town where volunteers handed out food. Word would travel fast in our network, especially when a member of the community froze to death.

I spent considerable time with homeless Vietnam veterans. The war itself was more than a half dozen years in the rearview mirror, but there were still plenty of vets on the street. I had met some vets in Los Angeles, but I came across even more in D.C. I learned a lot from them, and I urged other punks to join me in allying ourselves with the vets. They were on the streets with all kinds of physical and psychological problems, but they taught me lessons about how to live and survive, how to be my own person and stick up for myself, and how to be concerned about the plights of others. The punks had taught me how to get in trouble, rebel, reject, have fun without the fear of consequences, and be punk rock. The veterans taught me values I wouldn't otherwise have learned: military values that stuck with them despite the mental illnesses, some of which certainly would be diagnosed today as post-traumatic stress. By teaching me how to survive, they also taught me more than I had ever known about how to lead—lessons I still work each day to put into practice.

In my late teens, I bounced around more and spent some time living on the streets in New York City. New York was a rough, hard-core place to be a punk. (It was, at that time, a pretty rough, hard-core place to be anything.) I would hang out in Washington Square Park. The park is famous for its large stone arch built in the early twentieth century. In those days, when punk was beginning to yield to hip-hop and skater culture, the park was known as a gathering place for artists and non-conformists—along with some of the down and out. I honed my breakdancing there, adding a skill that became valuable in my panhandling pursuits.

It was in that park that I once met Jean-Michel Basquiat, a graffiti artist turned painter, whose works were then selling for tens of thousands of dollars. A *New York Times* article in 1985 called Basquiat's work "…a fine balance between seemingly contradictory forces: control and spontaneity, menace and wit, urban imagery and primitivism." To me, he was a compelling figure but he never registered as an artist of renown. He was a guy in the park sharing a joint. I didn't know at the time that there were parallels between our childhoods. Basquiat's parents divorced when he was seven. "I had very few friends," he told a writer from *Vanity Fair*. "There was nobody I could trust. I left home when I was fifteen. I lived in Washington Square Park. Of course my father minded. Jesus Christ!"

I also had no way to know, in that one fleeting meeting, that this man, who collaborated with Andy Warhol and was a friend of the artist and social activist Keith Haring, would become an influence on my artistic expression. Basquiat died from his addictions in the late summer of 1988. I got clean and sober in December 1988.

Painting helped save me; it is something I embraced as an outlet. Today, my art is inspired by the powerful images of suffering and salvation I witness during my animal rescue work. I paint these images, capturing their intensity, not only to process the impact these scenes have on me, but also to share the animals' stories with others and spread the message that our choices affect others. I typically add a rustic element to my work by painting on salvaged antique ceiling tins or other "found" objects to convey the idea that these animals, once forgotten, are able to reclaim the lives once stolen from them.

I recognize that I am in a unique position to save animals' lives through my work and also immortalize their souls through my paintings. I believe I have a responsibility to create a visual representation of the brutal suffering and raw hopelessness of animals who are victimized by humans. Seeing the degree and the myriad of abuses perpetrated on animals time and time again takes its toll, and I consider myself very fortunate to have this healthy, cathartic outlet.

Through my artwork, I have merged my two passions, animal rescue and painting, with my quest to educate the public about the abuses of animals that occur within the industries that profit from their suffering throughout the country and all over the world. I hope that by recreating the images of their suffering, with the animals at their most vulnerable and desperate, I can inspire people to use their personal and professional lives to join me in ending animal abuse and stopping at nothing until they suffer no more.

In New York, I had my first companion animal that I was totally responsible for: a pigeon I named Charlie. He came up to me one day, looking for food. He hung around and stayed around. He was very bold. He let me touch him, interact with him, pick him up, and put him on my lap. I took Charlie everywhere. Being a punk on the street, I didn't have a chance to wash my clothes often, so I would walk around with bird droppings on my shoulders.

For a time, several friends and I squatted in an abandoned movie theater on the Lower East Side. We woke one morning to see an Italian gang outside that clearly felt the theater was their property, not ours, and they were intent on taking it back. We needed to get out, and fast. There wasn't much to gather; we used our backpacks as pillows, and everything we needed was inside. But my friend Matt couldn't find his boots. (When you're living on the streets, taking your boots off at night is a mistake. It makes a rapid escape impossible.) The gang threw Matt's boots out the window and then tried to force us out a window. Matt fled, but I refused to leave. I didn't have Charlie. I was distraught. I wasn't going anywhere without Charlie. When I located the bird, I raced outside. Matt and I had run in opposite directions, but we quickly found each other. The only things we were missing were his boots. We walked around the building, searching until we located the footwear—inside a fenced lot guarded by a Doberman. It fell to me, the guy with his boots on, to hop the fence and retrieve the goods. I handed Charlie to Matt, and told Matt to throw a rock a distance away from the Doberman, to create a diversion. I climbed the barbed wire fence. As I came down, I ran to get the boots while the Doberman started coming for me. Just as I got back to the fence, he snapped and ripped my pants, but I made it over unscathed. Charlie was fine.

Being a good punk in New York, I had to have at least one piercing, and I did the job myself using a safety pin. It got infected, and badly so. The ear was huge and hurt like hell. I didn't know what to do. It wasn't like I had medical insurance. Walking down the street, still in agony, I saw a man in scrubs or a labcoat—something that looked medical. I asked him for advice. Surprisingly, he didn't bolt from me. He told me that a public hospital would have to treat me, that they couldn't send me away. So a friend and I walked to a hospital, along with Charlie. We sat in the waiting room for a long time. I had Charlie swaddled and on my lap, hidden from clear view. They eventually called my name—the fake name I gave them—and I quickly showed my companion how to wrap and hold Charlie.

I remember a nurse being genuinely concerned about my emaciated body and my general health. She remained interested—right up to the point that the doctor suggested she take me home and care for me. But the hospital did take care of my ear, and then they sent me on my way.

As I walked back into the waiting room, I encountered a frantic scene. Charlie was flying around the room. I had never before seen him take wing. People were swatting at the panicked bird with newspapers. I looked over at my friend who was supposed to be holding him. She was asleep. I managed to grab Charlie, shook my friend awake, and left the hospital, cursing at her as we went.

The hospital was bordered by a tall wrought iron fence that was covered on one side by ivy. As we walked outside, Charlie again took off and disappeared into the ivy on the other side of the fence. The only way I could get to him was to climb the fence.

I made it to the top and dug around gently. It took a few minutes, but I found Charlie. He was dead.

I don't think he had been injured in the waiting room fracas. Perhaps he was frightened to death. All I knew was that he had expired. It was one of the few times in my life, to that point, that I can remember having cried.

After my relatively short stint in New York came to an end, I returned to the streets of Washington, DC, where I met a girl, a punk kid a lot like me. Unlike me, she had a relationship with her parents, who seemed to like me. They lived in an upscale suburb in Maryland and didn't embrace the idea of their daughter hanging out with a homeless, jobless punk. They convinced their son Tony—a recovering addict—to give me a job as a laborer for his construction business. I worked building and renovating swimming pools and other concrete structures. I had a pretty strong work ethic, I discovered, and I started to develop a trade.

Tony knew I was anything but clean and sober, but even after Tony's sister and I broke up, he became my *de facto* brother, maybe even my father figure.

By the time I turned twenty, I had smashed up enough company trucks and done enough damage to him professionally that Tony said he was done with me, that I needed to get clean or get out. Out of options and feeling cornered, I agreed to try rehab. He was about to fire me, but Tony pledged to stand by me and hold my job for me.

I had health insurance through Tony's company, but it covered only a little more than half of the $20,000 rehab would cost. The counselor I worked with during admission ran through a list of people I could ask to help. The only one I couldn't rule out was my father. After an awkward phone call, the first one in years, he agreed to cover the shortfall.

I checked in on December 12, 1988. Most everyone who has become a recovering addict remembers her or his first day of sobriety. Some even have it tattooed on their arms. December 12 should have been my sobriety date, but I snuck a bottle of Jameson Irish Whiskey in with me. The date I remember, when I truly began my sobriety, was December 13.

I checked into the program at Suburban Hospital in Bethesda, Maryland, a short distance north of Washington, DC. I was in detox for eleven days, which was then an extended period. After detox, I was in rehab for a month. After that, I agreed to go into out-patient aftercare.

I spent much of 1989 and 1990 focusing on my recovery and working for Tony. I found places to stay in the Washington suburbs, mostly living with people who were also in the recovery process. It isn't an exaggeration to say I was learning how to live. I knew nothing. I was really still a child. I had denied myself every emotion. Now I was experiencing them all at once. Everything was bubbling to the surface. I needed aftercare to begin coping with it all.

During the first year of my sobriety, I attended twelve-step meetings two to three times a day. I realized I needed to do everything I was told to do, and I did recovery right. I embraced Alcoholics Anonymous. It became my lifeblood. If I wasn't working, I was in a meeting. If I wasn't in a meeting, I was having dinner with AA people.

Most twelve-step meetings are held in meeting halls in libraries, church basements, and the like. But there are also clubs: spaces local twelve-step organizations purchase or rent and dedicate to meetings. Just as I was getting clean, one of the first twelve-step clubs in the Washington area was just getting established. The Westside Club in the Georgetown section of Washington is one of the places I went to meetings. I would also attend twelve-step meetings in some of the less privileged sections of the city. They had a grittier atmosphere that I appreciated.

I entered The Westside Club at the side of the building, up a metal staircase. The club had four or five meeting rooms plus a little storefront counter where I could buy soft drinks and other refreshments. The place was continually filled with the odor of a pot of coffee that had been on the burner far too long.

It seemed that whenever I went to the Westside Club I showed up at the wrong time or ended up in the wrong room. It was a wrong turn that led to a turning point in my life. I entered the club one winter's evening and went to the first room on the right. It was crowded, with perhaps eighty to a hundred people in chairs and couches that formed a large square. I had to walk through several rows of people to get to a seat in the back by a wall. Wearing layers of winter clothes, I was immediately uncomfortable in the stuffed, crowded, overheated room. The meeting had just begun, but I was already sweating. My perspiration accelerated because this turned out to be a "Big Book" meeting. Formally titled *Alcoholics Anonymous*, the Big Book, first published in 1939, is the bible of AA. A Big Book meeting is just one kind of twelve-step meeting, and it is the kind I most tried to avoid.

A Big Book meeting normally involves using a passage as the topic for a moderated discussion. At this one, they were passing the Big Book from one person to another; each would read one paragraph. After that, the rest of the session would center around a discussion of recovery and how different people's experiences related to the reading.

With so many people in the room, I knew that one chapter was unlikely to require every person in the room to read aloud. I was banking on it. I tried to mathematically estimate the likelihood of getting stuck reading from this book. As it moved from one person's hands to another, my confidence grew. Some people would get on a roll and read more than one paragraph. The more time someone spent reading, the less likely it was I would have to read. Then things took an ugly turn; the book headed in my direction.

I was sweating in waves. The Big Book is written in language utterly unlike the way real people talk. Its language is formal, unfamiliar—like Shakespeare to a comic book reader. I never spent much time in school and my education, for all intents and purposes, had stopped at the fifth grade. Yes, I could understand words, but words on a page were just a jumble. I might have known a word, I might have known its meaning, but when I saw it in print, I didn't recognize it. And words I could read with my eyes were rarely words I could read aloud.

As I realized the Big Book was going to make it to me, I felt myself turning bright red. I was frozen in place. My heart was pounding. I considered bolting from the room, but that would have required climbing over people and making an annoyance of myself to a roomful of recovering addicts. It was pure paranoia at its worst.

The book landed in my lap. *Now I'm fucked*, I thought. The version of the Big Book being handed around was a hardback with a blue cover, not unlike the size or shape of a bible. As I held it, I knew I was trapped. I had no option but to start reading. As soon as I began, I felt that the words coming out of my mouth were nonsense, that no one in the room could understand me. In reality, I may have been more coherent than I believed, but at best I was fumbling and stumbling. My voice cracked. My hands shook. I had to stop. I couldn't continue. Trying to read just wasn't sustainable. I might have gotten through two sentences. I'm not sure.

I stopped, and I closed the book. I looked up and said, to no one in particular, "I'm terribly sorry. I can't comprehend the words in this book. I don't have the education to do so."

Then I began to cry.

Seconds later, I felt a warm hand on my right shoulder. The touch was an attempt by a stranger to tell me it was okay. With that gesture, I fell apart. Rather than feeling a sense of safety or security, I lost any composure I had remaining and began to sob.

I have no memory of what he said, but the meeting's moderator said something to get the attention off of me, and the meeting moved on. But I still felt I was the focal point of the whole room. I couldn't look at anyone, fearing each person in the room was staring at me. I had to sit and suffer through the meeting. All I wanted was to be invisible, for nobody to address me or look at me or even think about me. That was not going to happen.

As soon as the meeting ended, I found myself surrounded by an astounding group hug. I was embraced by dozens of people who had come together seeking encouragement in their journeys of sobriety, and no one judged me. No one had any expectations of me. They just wanted to help.

At that meeting, a group of people I didn't know well, people I knew only by first name, came together to teach me to read better and comprehend words. After AA meetings, a rotating group of people would take me to restaurants, their homes, or park benches, and tutor me.

Those people, who were doing the hard work of trying to change their own lives, changed my life. Their selfless willingness to fix a problem was among the most compassionate moments I can remember. Their kindness will always be etched in me.

That type of kindness still presents a challenge to me when I find someone panhandling. Handing out money to every homeless person I come across, especially in an urban area, is not sustainable, but I can't escape the fact that I once lived on the street, too. The panhandlers can never be obstacles or annoyances. They are people. I try to make eye contact with people panhandling, and I will talk to homeless people, hear their stories, and try to help them in very real ways.

Sometimes I try to help people meet their needs. A couple of years ago, I encountered a man and his dog living on a street in Los Angeles. I struck up a conversation with him, inquiring about his dog and how I could help. The man told me he was only asking for money to fund surgery his dog required. He told me about a car accident that started a spiral leading his family—his wife and dog—into homelessness. I gave him my time and my understanding, and I was convinced that his story was true. So I called one of my donors, one of my best friends and one of the most compassionate people with means I know, Chris Hoar. "You're the one person I thought would stand up and help him," I told Chris. So he did, and he paid for the surgery.

If I can help, I will. It's all about making my own decisions. Just like a proud punk.

CHAPTER FOUR

ANIMAL CONTROL

In 1990, I began tutoring sessions through a group called House of Hope, with the goal of passing tests to earn my high school equivalency diploma. Committing to intense study was a new experience for me, and for the first time, I began thinking about a future.

While I was considering my next moves, Washington, DC, was earning a new reputation, one that had nothing to do with presidents, famous buildings, Smithsonian museums, statues, or political squabbles. In 1990, Washington, DC, was America's murder capital. Gang wars and crack cocaine had turned parts of the city into places where no one was safe. "Almost every night, street scuffles end with a burst of gunfire, the shriek of sirens and yet another young black man turned corpse," wrote Bob Baker and Douglas Jehl in a lengthy story in the *Los Angeles Times*. "The blood bath is overwhelming. Drug peddlers kill competitors over a disrespectful stare. Rivals are executed in their car on a dark, heavily wooded street that was once a lovers' lane. High school boys eager to become 'hustlers' are shot to death while hanging out with the dealers they so admire. Shots are fired with chilling accuracy; there is little random spraying of gunfire." So prevalent was the violence that one local television station aired a program just after the late news each night called *City Under Siege*. It was rumored to be don't-miss television in the D.C. jail.

Washington lagged a few years behind New York and Los Angeles, where crack had become a problem in 1984. But Washington found a way to bring a drug epidemic to a symbolic crescendo in 1990, when Mayor Marion Barry became a national punchline after being caught by an FBI surveillance camera smoking crack in a hotel room.

It was in that city and that troubled year that I began thinking about doing something to make the world—or at least my city—better.

I had a close friend in Washington named Tracy whom I had met in rehab. She had lived in Oregon, and I referred to her as a crunchy granola type. She was determined to do something earthy, something valuable, something that would change society. I was spending some of my free time trying to help addicts on the street find food, shelter, and maybe treatment. I volunteered at a center for battered women, working with mothers and children who were abused, neglected, and homeless. I thought my focus was going to be helping children.

In the middle of our mutual recovery, Tracy began working for a national animal rights organization. She spoke to me often about issues and philosophies about animals and how we treat them. They were foreign notions, about ownership versus companionship, not consuming animals or using products derived from them, and humane sheltering and protection of stray animals. In the end, Tracy was responsible for my career, for the animals I have saved over the years.

Tracy raised the possibility of my going to work for the Washington Humane Society, which was hiring. WHS, as it is often known, has a storied history that began with a Congressional charter in 1870. In the early nineties, as now, it managed animal control for the city. Tracy had connections and put in a good word for me. I was sufficiently intrigued to pursue the job, which could have been mine, save for one obstacle: It required a high school diploma.

My tutoring through House of Hope stretched to more than six months. I had a lot of catching up to do. I was thoroughly taken aback the day my instructor called me over and simply said, "You're ready for the test."

No way, I thought. I'm not close to ready. But I took the exam. I passed.

Equivalency diploma in hand, I applied for and got the job of animal control officer with WHS.

Back then there was no formal training. You just spent several weeks or months under a senior animal control officer, and then they released you onto the street. The objective was to get you out and taking calls as soon as possible. It was always an underfunded program. There were only five animal control officers in the city. Because we worked in shifts, at peak times, we had just two on the street, dividing Washington, DC into east and west. We were paid peanuts. But I think they bred quality animal control officers because of the philosophical mentality they put into us, which was heavily influenced by the longstanding affiliation between WHS and People for the Ethical Treatment of Animals. I was a hard worker, and I worked until the work was done. I quickly embraced the opportunity and the responsibility of rewriting the destiny of animals.

One of my first abuse cases involved a sacrificial séance. Arriving at the scene, I found a goat nailed to a wooden cross and several chickens with their heads recently severed. I immediately called in law enforcement, seized the several remaining living chickens, and euthanized other animals who were suffering and near death. When I returned to the shelter at the end of a very long day to unload my van and do my paperwork, I asked my shift supervisor what would happen to the chickens. She said they would be put to death. That certainly wasn't the answer I sought. *Why*, I wondered, reverting to free-thinking punk rocker mode, *did I save them just so we could kill them?* "Are there any other options?" I asked. She told me about an animal sanctuary about an hour outside of the city, but that she had no way of getting them there. Naturally, my response was, "I'll get them there." She agreed, and an hour later I was off delivering those chickens to a farm sanctuary with the promise of a life free from any further suffering or danger of being killed by human hands.

On the way to the sanctuary, I took the opportunity to grab a quick bite to eat, and without even considering the irony of what I was doing, pulled into the drive-through of a Kentucky Fried Chicken restaurant.

Then the light bulb went off. Even though that nicely packaged box of fried bird in front of me bore no resemblance to the chickens in the back of my van, I could no longer lie to myself. I could no longer ignore the obvious. The connection couldn't have been any clearer that there was no difference between the chickens I had worked so hard to bring to safety and the ones I was so willing to consume. On that spot, at that fast food restaurant, I vowed to live a vegan way of life from then on. Only later did I learn about the severity of suffering and abuse chickens endured on their way to that box on my lap. I stopped eating animals purely out of concern for them. In the years since, my health and my conscience have been the beneficiaries.

It is important to note that the WHS I am describing, from the early 1990s, was typical of its time. WHS has continued to evolve and to seek higher standards. Sadly, too many of today's shelters across the United States have not moved forward from earlier times.

In a small, underfunded operation like WHS, in an often-dangerous big city, humane standards in animal control in the early 1990s were certainly not ubiquitous. People cut corners and some of the practices at WHS were less than optimal. The best of humane intentions by many were overwhelmed by the stresses of a shelter filled to capacity on a daily basis. It was becoming a capture-and-kill operation. Every day, forty to fifty animals were being put to death to make way for new animals coming in. The grim selection process put pit bulls and black dogs first in line for death.

I once got into an argument with my supervisor about just that type of issue. I had brought in a litter of pups and their mother.

They were surrendered, not seized or stray, so we were able to put them up for adoption right away. The mother was black. Three of the puppies were black, and three were tan. The day after I brought them to the shelter, I went to check on them. The three tan puppies were there, and the black ones were gone.

"Where are the black puppies?" I asked my supervisor.

"I euthanized them," she answered. "To make space."

I understood the philosophy that black dogs were less desirable. But I summoned my courage to question her.

"But you didn't actually create space for more dogs. They were all in the same run. They're all still in the same run. There are just fewer animals in the same space."

She reiterated that the black ones would be less desirable for adoption than the tan ones.

"But they weren't taking up any space," I insisted. "It's not like by killing the black dogs, you cleared a run."

The conversation was futile. I couldn't bring the three puppies back to life. We weren't going to come to any resolution, but the viewpoint of leadership was clear. It was the kind of incident that helped shape the beliefs I later put into practice and still advocate across animal sheltering.

The call volume for our department was so high we could never catch up. I would start each day responding to calls written in a ledger. During the day, more calls would come in over the radio. We always had a backlog. On busy days, we had to prioritize. Lost animals, sick animals, even abused animals had to wait for animals hit by cars and other immediate life-and-death situations.

One of my cases was not far from the animal shelter and my office, in the Trinidad section of Washington, DC. It was then, as it is now, a neighborhood where caution ought to rule the day. The call came in with a report that a dog was being beaten with a piece of two-by-four lumber on the front stoop of a rowhouse. I jumped in my van and virtually jetted over, thanks to lighter than usual early-evening traffic. It probably took me five minutes to get there.

The dog was a wire-haired terrier mix. The woman who lived in the home had the dog on a chain-link leash with a leather handle. The leash was tied to the banister. As I pulled up, the woman was still hitting the dog. A kid, a teenager, was in the middle of the street. He flagged me down and came running up to my window, shouting, "There's that bitch. There she is. She's beating her dog. Go stop that bitch." He was a kid in the middle of a tough neighborhood who was incredibly upset by the fact that somebody was hurting an animal. That meant a lot to me. I was just beginning to understand the city, how animals and people lived alongside each other. I remember feeling a lot of hope for that kid who had little or nothing to his name but was concerned about an animal.

I went running up to the stoop. "Ma'am," I said, "drop the board." Instead, she raised the board over her head and swung at me. I blocked it with my hand, knocked her down, and radioed for police assistance. Fortunately, the officers arrived quickly. My immediate objective was to secure the dog and figure out everything else after that. The woman was screaming at me, and neighbors were screaming at her. I unchained the dog and took him to my van.

Once the woman and the dog were secured and separated from each other, I couldn't resist asking, "Ma'am, why on earth were you out there beating your dog?"

"Let me show you," she responded. She took me in the house and showed me some plastic moulding with teeth marks in it. "The dog chewed the fucking moulding off of my wall while I was at work today."

"So that's why you beat your dog?"

"Well, yeah, I gotta teach him."

I took him to the vet for medical care and then to the shelter soon after. He was adopted into a loving home.

I was fortunate to work my first job as an animal control officer for a humane society that, despite some practices I disagreed with, was greatly influenced in other ways by an animal protection attitude. Ingrid Newkirk, PETA's leader then and today, had played a leadership role in the Washington Humane Society. She and others were instrumental in obtaining for WHS the Washington, DC, contract to do animal control. My initial education and my on-the-job training were from an animal protection perspective, as opposed to an animal control perspective. We responded to a call about an animal in distress because of the animal, not because he was a perceived nuisance. If a wild animal was trapped on someone's property, I would release the animal. Just because they're rodents, for example, doesn't mean they don't have the right to live life freely.

That wasn't the perspective of most Washingtonians, and certainly not the general perspective of animal control in most parts of the United States. But the organization I worked for ingrained that philosophy in me. It continues to influence me.

I once had a rat-in-a-toilet call to the home of an elderly woman on Capitol Hill. I went in. She was freaked out. I opened the lid. Sure enough, the rat was in the toilet. I had my thick, heavy protective gloves on. I grabbed him and headed outside.

"What are you doing to do?" she asked.

"I'm going to take him outside and release him."

"*What*? Why on earth would you do that?"

"Because he's wildlife, and he belongs in the wild."

"Why wouldn't you kill him?"

"There's nothing wrong with him."

I wasn't going to engage in more conversation. I got where she was coming from, and there was no way she was going to get where I was coming from. So I walked outside. I saw her looking out her window. I went off to the side of the house in the bushes, and I released him. A day later there was a newspaper article about city animal control not doing its job, releasing rodents back into the population.

I did some of everything: police raids, squirrels in chimneys, a puppy stuck in a drain pipe, dogs abandoned in fleabag motels, dogs protecting drug dealers, monkeys in apartments, alligators being walked in city streets. During a Grateful Dead concert at Robert F. Kennedy Stadium on a steaming hot summer day, I had a call to a giant parking lot full of hundreds of dogs left in cars. I impounded an incredible number of dogs that day. We just went in and swept that place.

With every call I went on, in every interaction, I learned more and more about how to put compassion into practice. But it wasn't just for animals. I met a skinny little kid named Gary. He was probably six or seven years old and was running on the streets in the Adams Morgan neighborhood where I lived. Gary's mother was impoverished and living with numerous challenges. He was a good kid whose life could have been on a sad but familiar trajectory. So I took him under my wing. Gary became my unofficial child. He went everywhere with me. I clothed him. We went to thrift shops to make the most of my meager spending money.

Gary was jumped one day, or so his mother told me. They took his winter jacket, she said, in what I am certain was a cover story. More than likely she had taken the jacket and sold it. Not long after that, she moved him to the projects in a far worse part of town where drugs were more plentiful. We lost touch when I moved away from Washington several years later. I felt guilty, but also felt that I had done something right with him. I now know that he is still in the Washington area and is a devoted father.

I answered a lot of calls in the southeast portion of D.C., in dangerous streets and neighborhoods. I was shot at several times. The first was a call for a Rottweiler running loose. It was a relatively benign call and not a priority. I got to the house and spotted the dog, who bolted for the back. Neighbors on the porch began screaming at me and screaming at the dog, urging him to attack me—which he did. The woman next door continued screaming, telling me I had no business in her neighborhood, and certainly no business telling her what to do. She called for someone. A big guy came out, and she told him to make me go away. He ducked inside, and came back out firing. I dove into the van and radioed in a "shots fired" call. Police were on the scene quickly and a few minutes later I received a "we got him" call. The cops put me in a squad car and drove me back to the scene to identify the subject, which I did. Back in the car, the officer turned into a park, shut off the lights on his vehicle, turned to me and said, "One less nigger on the street."

I was pissed. On one hand, I was grateful to be alive and not have a bullet hole anywhere in me, but I couldn't let this go. For me, there was no camaraderie that day. I went back and got the dog. I went on to other calls. And then I turned in that officer.

There were so many difficult calls that I can't recall them all. But it doesn't take much to make them start flooding back: an apartment building filled with squatters and animals; six pit bulls who had been in an apartment for a week with a corpse; and hundreds more.

During my time as an animal control officer, PETA sent interns to WHS to go on ride-alongs. On one of the more memorable nights, we got a call about a bloody pit bull in front of a building in one of the toughest neighborhoods in town. We got to the address, but saw no sign of the dog. We drove around the building and were taking one last pass when two guys emerged from the building with a pit bull. Watching from the van, we could see no blood or obvious injuries on the dog. I decided the call was a write-off. When I looked back up to the street, though, I could see only one of the two men. I started the engine and, before pulling out, made a check of the outside mirror on the right. There I caught sight of the second man aiming a pistol at the van. He fired a number of rounds. I threw the van in park and started to jump out to confront the shooter. I was unarmed. The ride-along yelled at me to get in the truck and get away. I thought better of my original reactionary decision and tore out, flying down the street until we found a well-lighted gas station where I could assess the situation. I needed to look at the dogs in the back. One dog, whom I had performed a field euthanasia on earlier in the evening after he was hit by a car, had a bullet hole in his body. The living dogs were unharmed. My ride-along emerged from the van and came around to the back. He was dressed in khaki pants—with a large wet spot on the front. No doubt, it was an educational evening for him, but unfortunately, one with little opportunity to practice compassionate animal control.

And then there was the person we called Voodoo Man. In his fifties with graying dreadlocks, ratty robe, and a cane adorned with bones, Voodoo Man made an impression, to say the least. We dealt with him on more than a few cases. He was irresponsible with animals. He also killed animals for his rituals and séances. I once picked up his dog, a mixed terrier, as a stray. I wasn't at the shelter when he retrieved his dog, but my boss, who was, said, "That guy scared the shit out of me." Voodoo Man also told my boss he had put a curse on me. More than once I had to investigate Voodoo Man for animal cruelty. After one of those investigations, he told me he was going to curse me again, and bad things would happen if I went back to his property. Despite the warning, I went back to his residence on a subsequent investigation. I found fresh animal parts on his lawn, leading to an unlocked shed. I knocked and got no answer. I opened the shed door, thinking there could be a dead or dying animal inside. I found no animal. What I did find, though, was a bowl filled with blood, in front of a lit candle. In the bowl was a piece of paper; scrawled on it was a note that simply said, "Officer Haisley." Given the fact that I am still here and functioning, I can only assume Voodoo Man's curse was ineffective.

In my four years as an animal control officer in the nation's capital, every day was a learning opportunity—about care and compassion for animals, about the best and the worst of humanity, about tools and techniques to deal with any situation I might encounter. I was fortunate to be exposed to progressive philosophies about how to do my job. And I learned from experience that working in animal control can make you a public target.

What made me most effective was that I pushed past roadblocks. I had to be resourceful, which meant I often had to ask others to jump in and help. I had to utilize every resource available. I had to be authoritative. I had to be situational, a bit of a chameleon. One minute I was dealing with drug dealers in a raid where police knew, in addition to the drugs, we would encounter a bunch of pit bulls. I would face attacking dogs and flying bullets. The next minute I would be in a wealthy neighborhood responding to a house where Chelsea Clinton was visiting that had an uninvited raccoon in the backyard.

In 1994, an international animal protection group sent a task force to take over a municipal shelter in Ponce, Puerto Rico. They asked me to help lead that mission and convinced WHS to keep me on the payroll while I traveled for a month. On the ground in Ponce, which is in the south of Puerto Rico, we found a dilapidated, vastly overtaxed shelter with massive outbreaks of Canine Parvovirus, which is better known as Parvo, and distemper, which are highly contagious viruses. In dealing with the epidemics, as well as the incredible overcrowding of an inadequate facility, the organization I was assisting wound up euthanizing sick animals and putting to death hundreds of others suspected to be sick. The resources in Puerto Rico were limited, at best. That is not the way one might operate today, when there are ways to treat some sick animals and methods of getting at least some of the other dogs to adoption partners.

I intentionally draw a distinction between putting animals to death and euthanasia. Euthanasia is a Greek word variously translated as "the good death," "easy death," or "merciful death." Dictionaries generally define euthanasia as the process of inducing a painless death to alleviate pain and suffering. Without a doubt, in my world, euthanasia is sometimes necessary, a gift legally available only to animals in most U.S. states. We rescue animals who are simply too sick or injured to have a reasonable chance of survival or any quality of life. We euthanize to relieve suffering. It is a somber choice but a responsible one.

There are, however, animal shelters, public and private, across the United States and beyond that give lethal injections to animals for many reasons not related to suffering. Overcrowded shelters put dogs and cats to death because they need space or because staff members believe in the antiquated notion that a dark-colored dog or an older cat could never be adopted. Some subscribe to the belief that certain breeds of dogs are inherently dangerous and are not suitable candidates for adoption, so they are routinely put to death.

None of those situations constitutes euthanasia. Yet I choose not to refer to them by a more accusatory term like "murder" or "killing." Using harsh terms to discuss practices I disagree with—and work to change—doesn't lead to open discussion or resolution. I choose a more neutral, yet factual, term of "put to death." Getting past finger-pointing terms is part of the mission of humane and compassionate education, as my colleagues and I practice it.

It also bears mentioning that while I challenge easy assumptions that lead to deaths, I do not use the widely misused term "no-kill." Our guardianship of the animals we rescue is a responsibility, which can lead to difficult choices we would rather not make. But they are choices that, in my view, are part of a humane view. (More on that later.) Space needs, age, color, treatable illness, and "bad" breeds do not fit the definition of euthanasia; they are not merciful deaths. But I believe that making difficult, responsible decisions about merciful death is part of the mantle of compassion.

In our brief time in Puerto Rico, we also worked to clean up the place, begin designing a new shelter, and training staff and volunteers how to maintain standards.

When I returned from Puerto Rico, I was given an award and a party. It was the first time I had been around so many like-minded people, and the fact that they appreciated my efforts made it all the sweeter. In the weeks and months that followed, word about the Ponce mission had spread through the animal welfare and animal rights communities, and I began to get a reputation as someone who could take on a challenge and get the job done. My work on the D.C. streets had taught me immeasurable lessons, but Puerto Rico put me on the map.

I happily returned to what I considered the best job in the world: waking up and saving lives. But I also had become a target. When you shine, you sometimes make other people look bad, and some are happy to call you a grandstander. After four years on the job, I knew my stuff, and I was largely able to ignore my detractors. *You're talking but I'm working*, I thought. The truth is that it hurts when stories came back to me, often in particularly inaccurate retellings. But it was mostly envy-based. I worked damn hard, and I got some notice out of it.

I got a call one day in 1995 from a headhunter in New York who was working on behalf of the city's newly formed Center for Animal Care and Control. After more than a century of running the animal shelters for New York City, The American Society for the Prevention of Cruelty to Animals had recently chosen not to renew its contract. The city had hastily placed shelter management under the auspices of the semi-independent Center, which was supervised by the Department of Health. The headhunter asked if I was interested in running the Manhattan shelter, the "flagship location," the one most eyes were following. I went up and interviewed. I had misgivings about taking on all of the administrative duties that would be involved and about my qualifications to manage staff members, but I was ready for a change and found myself intrigued by the opportunity to create the most dynamic humane operation in the country. It was going to be an outsized challenge, but I jumped in.

"Animal control in New York City is a nightmare," wrote Elizabeth Hess in a *Village Voice* exposé that laid bare just how bad our problems were. "On an average day, hundreds of unwanted animals are born, hundreds die, and a few lucky ones enter a shelter and survive. Most New Yorkers don't have a clue that their city is responsible for one of the worst animal surplus problems in the country; we take in roughly 60,000 dogs, cats, and wilder creatures a year. And that's the good news. Without a shelter system, these animals and discarded pets would die painful, often slow deaths."

I got the job and went to New York to change the world.

Before I left D.C., my last call was for a pit bull shot in the head. I found the dog at two in the morning. He was clearly the loser of a semi-organized dogfight and had been executed with a single shot. I arrived at a vacant lot where his body lay, at about the same time the police did. His wounds were still fresh. All I could do was collect the remains. When you pride yourself on rescuing animals, it is particularly dispiriting when circumstances make it impossible to help. I had been privileged to make positive changes for animals and people who lived in our nation's capital while at WHS. But it was time to see a new place and take on a new mission.

I lasted a year at the Center for Animal Care and Control. I quickly realized I wasn't hired to make change but to shut people up. They wanted someone with a humane reputation whose presence, they believed, would silence very vocal critics of their shoddy operation.

The initial budget for the Center's shelter operations was $4.5 million, an amount the ASPCA had claimed was inadequate. The Center's executive director had no previous animal shelter management, and the board chair of the Center for Animal Care and Control was the Commissioner of Sanitation, which the Shelter Reform Action Committee deemed "a crudely stark admission that the City views homeless animals as garbage."

Media coverage of the Center focused in large part on the number of animals it put to death, prompting one City Council member to declare the Center a "little animal Auschwitz."

Inflammatory language aside, the problems were deep: structural issues, such as inadequate ventilation and drainage; staff members with criminal animal abuse records; injured animals brought in overnight left unattended; dogs and cats placed in adjoining cages; cages that ensnared dogs' paws and snouts.

Although I charged in ready to make change on behalf of the animals, it became clear very quickly that I wasn't going to get anything I needed from the city administration. It was a purely bureaucratic operation; there was no interest in improvement, just in the illusion of it.

Frustrating as that job was, I still learned from it. I had worked in and around shelters, but I had never run one. I immersed myself in trying to understand sheltering from the inside and to develop my own ideas on how it could be made better. In one of my more extreme experiments, I tried to experience life in an animal shelter from an animal's perspective. I put myself in a cage for twenty-four hours. It was a stacked unit with three dogs in their own cages over my head. My section was six feet wide, three feet deep, and three feet high. It barely fit my body. I am six feet, one inch tall and weighed one hundred eighty-five pounds. I could not fully stretch, could barely turn around, and certainly could not stand. I had a volunteer provide me basic food and water, but just the basics. At the end of the workday, the staff turned the lights off. Everybody went home. I was amazed, when all of my rights had been taken away, by how fast my psyche was affected. I couldn't do anything that came naturally to me. In that single day, I could feel my physical health being affected. More than anything, I wanted to stretch, to stand up, to go where I wanted to go. I longed for all of the things I didn't have, even the simplest ones. Of course, I was not a dog. I related to everything from a human perspective. The true experience of being a dog is something we can only imagine, but I felt as though I was beginning to comprehend the barrier rage animals in cages so often develop.

I gave Manhattan my best shot. I fought for changes, but the frustrations piled high, and successes were rare. I needed to get out. So I quit—and publicly at that. I invited members of the news media to visit the shelter and see with their own eyes the conditions. If I was going to burn bridges, I decided to do so as loudly as I knew how.

"I spent time with Haisley his last week in the shelter," wrote Elizabeth Hess. "He was constantly in need of supplies; he pointed out backed-up sewage pipes in kennels swamped with feces, broken ventilation systems, damaged cages, and numerous problems that have been plaguing his staff, and the animals, for a year."

In the article, Hess quoted me saying, "I couldn't get even the most basic problems fixed. The building is falling apart. The cages are falling apart. Nobody in there is doing anything about it."

The way I left the Manhattan job was a risk I never really calculated. It might have killed my chances of working in animal sheltering, but it actually had the opposite effect. My reputation as someone who cared about—and would fight for—animals continued to grow.

I interviewed for shelter jobs in Houston and Longmont, Colorado, as a shelter director, and in San Mateo, California, as captain of humane law enforcement. I chose California because I wanted to get back to rescue work and addressing animal cruelty.

The job required considerable training. I graduated from a modified police academy after a series of courses, as well as the California state humane academy. As an officer, I carried a sidearm.

I stayed in the San Mateo job for just under two years. I was still finding my own way, developing myself and my own principles, and continuing to make a positive difference for the animals of my community and beyond. One of my first cases in San Mateo was to shut down an entire pet store.

And then I took away the firearms from my staff. As a humane officer, showing up with a gun—a .357 in a holster—automatically makes you intimidating, but it may make a humane mission less clear. You're not exactly screaming compassion. So I took away guns from a unit of people, many of whom were using animal control as a steppingstone to becoming police officers. They thought I was taking them backwards, hurting their careers. I had long-term goals for a humane system, not short-term ambitions of promotion. I had no interest in just doing a job. I wanted to change the world, even if the world was just one community. Eventually I realized San Mateo wasn't the place for me to change the world. But while I firmly believe we took steps I was unable to take in

Manhattan, I was hamstrung by a workforce that didn't share the same goals.

I decided to take some time off from the animal world. I took art classes and pursued a degree in the administration of justice at San Francisco Community College. But I wanted more. I could read and write; education had become, for me, a beautiful thing—English, math, history. For the first time in my life, school was fulfilling—until the animal protection world called me back.

I spent some time in India helping spearhead operations in Mumbai, Hyderabad, and Aurangabad. Our mission was to infiltrate the slaughter trade and the meat transport trade. I also traveled to animal shelters and sanctuaries, helping set higher care standards, applying grants and other funds to instill more humane attitudes in those shelters. Some of the most rewarding moments in my life and career were training people, showing that when you capture and handle an animal with patience, skill, and compassion, it is far more effective, not to mention more humane, than beating him with a stick.

India was also a practical education in how people and animals were forced to coexist in close quarters. I learned about the commonalities between ways we house dense populations of people and animals—and some of the ways we might do a better job at both.

Having worked in animal sheltering for the better part of a decade, in difficult, often unruly places with antiquated philosophies and policies, my time in New York and California, coupled with my experiences in India and Puerto Rico, sparked me to think much more deeply if there might be a better way to approach the notion of human sheltering—to think outside the cage.

Right after I returned to the U.S., I received a call to come back to Washington to run the animal control department at Washington Humane, which I did for two years. The job was familiar; with more authority, I did everything I could to make a smooth, efficient, and effective operation.

During this second stint at the Washington Humane Society, I had more responsibility and a more progressive mindset than ever before. But I never forgot the most basic principles about animals and the fact that I worked for them.

One emergency call from those days has particularly stayed with me. It was in northeast Washington, in a neighborhood that was dicey but not the worst the city had to offer. Part industrial, part residential, it also included a number of budget, chain motels that catered to tourists who likely would have stayed somewhere else, had they known more about the area. I was in the office when a radio call summoned me to the intersection of New York Avenue and Bladensburg Road.

A family vacationing from California had been in an accident. A tractor-trailer ran a red light and plowed into them. The entire family was in the car, including their German Shepherd. The father died on impact. When I arrived, his body was still in the street, covered with a white sheet. His daughter also lay on the street, in dire condition. The son and mother were not hurt. No one had seen the dog since he fled the vehicle.

Some cases hit me harder than others. To see the devastation—the shocked survivors, the bodies in the street—shook me up. What I wanted more than anything was to do right by that family and reunite them with one piece of their shattered lives. I was there for the dog. But, as I had come to understand more and more thoroughly, I was there for the family, too.

There were sightings over the next few days. I made each of those a priority. I remained on call after my shifts were over. I saw the dog twice in the ensuing days, but I wasn't able to catch him.

I went to the hospital to talk to the mother, who was still reeling from the loss of her husband and the decimation of her family, and I told her how much the case had affected me. I asked if she would join me in the van after a sighting, so she could call the dog's name in a familiar voice. Within a day, there was a new sighting. I raced to pick up the mother and took her to the location of the report. There was no sign of the dog. We trudged through an overgrown field. She called his name over and over. As we were about to give up, I caught sight of him, as if in slow motion, darting out of a wooded area, heading straight to her.

The reunion brought that grief-stricken woman back together with a precious member of her family. It didn't make the tragedy go away, but it reunited two companions, human and animal, who needed each other.

For years, I had been all about the animals, but this case reminded me that both people and animals were the keys to the change I hoped to create.

In 2001, the opportunity to help animals, to create a shelter built from the animals' perspective, to help create lasting family bonds with animals, came to me. This time, I was determined to turn a chance into a lasting solution.

CHAPTER FIVE

WASHINGTON ANIMAL RESCUE LEAGUE

The building that houses the Washington Animal Rescue League sits a few hundred feet into the northwest quadrant of the District of Columbia, four miles north of the U.S. Capitol, in a working class neighborhood of brick rowhouses. The League, or WARL, is just up the block from a graffiti-covered subway overpass in a pocket of brick industrial buildings, located across the street from a community garden where cornstalks and sunflowers pop up in the summer.

WARL's building is long and low, with an exterior façade of red brick with a sharply sloped green metal roof and a clock tower at one end. Inside the ring of Roman numerals, the clocks' faces are adorned with the League's logo: overlapping silhouettes of a dog and cat. At a glance from the street, the clock tower is the only thing that reveals the League's mission.

The three-story lobby is polished brick and wood, open and airy, softly lit by skylights and lamps. To the left, as you enter, is a veterinary suite; to the right are picture windows with views into puppy and cat showcase enclosures.

WARL is the District of Columbia's oldest animal shelter, dating to 1914. The shelter initially had a focus on horses; it expanded to dogs and cats, thanks to the widespread use of automobiles. In all of its history, WARL had been managed by its board of directors, without the leadership of an executive director.

The League approached me about becoming its first executive director, which set into motion a brief process capped by a final interview with members of the board of directors at the home of the owner of a chain of car dealerships. This was not exactly my natural environment, but years of working with the public had prepared me to positively interact with most any audience. I was hired.

WARL, at that time, wasn't unlike many of today's "no-kill" shelters. They took in dogs and cats and then put them in cages—without a plan—and just kept them there. Dogs and cats were adopted out at a dispiriting rate. For the most part, they were left to languish and decline. When I got there, WARL had fifty dog cages and an equal number of cat cages, each of which housed a single animal. There was no room to bring in more, and rarely did an animal leave. There was an adoption here or there, and occasionally one of several non-profit "rescue" groups of questionable mission and capabilities would pick up a group of dogs or cats. WARL had no educational programs. The Washington Animal Rescue League was doing a disservice to its animals and to the community. It was a warehouse for dogs and cats. Like so many other shelters in the United States, it had created barriers: literal barriers for the animals and emotional barriers for potential adopters, created by dismal conditions, when it should have created an environment of embrace. Behind that lovely lobby were row after row of cages, unsanitary conditions, a penetrating smell of ammonia, and animals who had given up.

WARL sought me out because its board realized the shelter needed change. I give them great credit for realizing the old ways were unsustainable. The League's board did a good job of funding current operations, but there was no consistent leadership. Suffice it to say that when I started the job, I was more than aware that I had inherited a mess.

I hadn't been looking for a job. I had been quite happy heading up animal control at the Washington Humane Society. I got up in the morning and rescued animals and trained and managed a team of officers of high caliber. What more could I want? So when WARL approached me, my first thought was, *Why would I want to work for an organization that has too much money, doesn't do anything good with that money for the animals, and keeps animals too long in a shelter environment, to the point that they ruin them?*

As soon as I asked myself that question, I knew that I needed to take the job. It was a shelter full of problems that I knew in my gut I would be able to fix, that it was a place to create a lasting solution.

As I mentioned, WARL was a stereotypical animal shelter. The main dog room was about seventy-five feet long and sixty feet wide. The floor was concrete and the ceiling was open, leading up to the skylights—which were unique for a shelter, a welcome bit of light that didn't come from a fluorescent tube. The floor space was filled with cages: steel uprights with chain-link panels.

When you put dogs and cats in cages, about the only beneficial thing you have accomplished is to restrict them from running loose. But suddenly these social species are isolated and imprisoned. When they are in cages, dogs decline rapidly, and they decline in several predictable phases.

The first is logical and understandable: rage. We call it cage rage or barrier rage. When you put a dog behind steel bars or chain link fencing, you create a barrier, a jail cell. Dogs can look through the bars and see other dogs or people, whom they can't reach. Not being able to get to them, not being able to have any social interaction, they react with piercing, sustained barking. In a kennel or shelter situation, with row after row of dogs eyeing each other, their anxiety builds as each new prisoner joins the chorus of distressed noise. The situation becomes one of massive negative stimulation. Not only will dogs bark; many will lunge and growl at the front of the cage. This can happen to the sweetest, friendliest dog in the world. At that point, a potential adopter walking through won't see the real dog. That dog may not be truly aggressive, but in that cacophonous situation of communal rage, he appears to be. The truth is that many dogs are merely reacting to the environment. But how could you tell?

The tyranny of the cage next manifests into what, in human terms, we would call depression—or a lessened interest in life. Dogs move to the back of their cages. They become disinterested and start to shut down. The timeframe of this stage differs in individual dogs. It may take days, weeks, or months. While dogs may go to the back of their cages, seemingly sullen and depressed, they may still lunge at someone walking by. The true nature of that dog is hidden. He doesn't want to play. He may not take a treat from your hand. He just exists.

I have seen dogs in this depressed stage succumb to death. At best, they become vacant. Attempts to walk them or give them any form of enrichment fail because the only reaction they seem capable of showing an approaching person is disinterest or aggression.

The last and most disconcerting stage of decline is the potentially permanent compromise of a dog's mental health. It often begins as self-mutilation—a dog attacking himself—and in evermore out-of-control aggression. A caretaker walking into the cage to change food or water may be attacked. And then dogs begin to spin—not merely running in circles, they turn in the tiniest of circles, making rotation after uncontrolled rotation. It is an obsessive-compulsive behavior I have rarely seen corrected, at least in the environment that created it. The dog's psyche—again borrowing a human term—has been affected. If the dog can be helped at this point, it will take tremendous, patient rehabilitation at the direction of a trainer who specializes in animal behavior.

Caged cats also decline in a shelter environment, but they do so differently from dogs. Dogs are emotional, social creatures. Cats are more tidy, independent animals, social in their own unique ways. In too many shelters, cats are forced into cages two feet by two feet by two feet: a steel box with a cage front, with a litter box taking up a big part, if not the majority, of that space. The cages often have no perches or scratching posts, which are vital for their enrichment. In those cages, we strip away their chances to be independent and curious. Their decline often manifests in a compromised immune system. They become sick or take on chronic medical issues, and they spread disease. At that point, you have a cat room full of sick cats. A sneezing cat is a common reason used by many shelters to put them to death, to avoid an outbreak.

Sadly, all of these steps of decline remain common in today's sheltering, and the biggest culprit is the cage.

Animal sheltering has made many advancements in recent years, but the continuation of insufficient funding, inadequate construction, lack of vision, and poor leadership set up the potential adopters, the animals, and those charged with their care for failure.

A well-run animal shelter is equal parts physical structure, leadership, proactive programs, and driving philosophy. Philosophy has to drive mission, and mission has to drive action. But it starts with guiding principles, with philosophy. So often, animal shelters operate because someone started them decades ago, and a succession of people have come along and followed instructions. No one asked why. No one asked if there might be a better way. The shelters' guiding principles, which may have made sense twenty or thirty years ago, do not make sense today.

Unfortunately, there aren't enough progressive leaders driven by compassion who have appropriate knowledge and experience. Too many in the animal sheltering field are unable to strike a crucial balance between business and compassion. People adopt for emotional reasons. And people work in shelters for emotional reasons. Those are the people you want working for animals. But as a leader you have to create a marriage between emotion and business—and then walk a fine line between the two; for it is that emotion, that sympathy, and that concern that are the essence of compassion.

Caring people across the United States and beyond do their best to meet the needs of animals in shelters, but our animal shelter system is broken. For most people, animal shelters summon visions of dark, dingy, dirty places where animals wait in fear and loneliness until they are put to death. Too often that remains the case. The fear created by that stereotype is what I believe is the greatest impediment to more widespread animal adoption.

Traditional shelters made of cages work against our mission of finding permanent, loving homes. It is a fixable problem—not solely fixed through programs, policies, education, attitudes, or operations. The building, the physical structure, is crucial to the solution. If the building is not up to par, you're simply putting a bandage on a bigger problem and as a result, creating more problems.

That's why so many shelter organizations have tried to sugarcoat their conditions by building lofty entryways, using decorative tiles in the dog runs, or painting the cat room with an aesthetically pleasing palette. But the fact is, the animals remain in the same tired, failed environment of cages. They may be updated, nicer cages, but they remain barriers. You can still see the despair in the animals and almost feel it in the air. The shelter is not a community center of any kind. It is a place of lost hope, not a place that shows life has value, where there is dignity for all, where there is hope, where animals can thrive.

WARL was very definitely sugarcoated.

The Washington Animal Rescue League that I stepped into lacked any plans or programs. The shelter was well-meaning but typical in its disorganization, dirt, and depression. Sixty percent of its dogs were spinning in their cages.

No one was operating WARL from a business perspective. Nor had there ever been anyone in a leadership role with experience in animal protection or animal sheltering. There was no coordination of decisions. There was no leadership, no management of staff members, and no master plan. What WARL needed wasn't a plan, but triage.

I first needed to stop the bleeding, to make immediate changes that would improve sanitation and the most basic of conditions for the animals. We had fifty dog runs containing fifty decaying dogs—dogs who had declined emotionally, socially, and physically. One of the first things I did—one of the easiest, best, and cheapest things any organization can and should be doing for its animals—was provide them opportunities to interact. I began allowing compatible dogs to spend time with each other. The staff was blown away. Dogs who would bite you if you went in their cages became dogs who began to play, because we allowed them to be social.

Dogs, by nature, need to be part of a social system. They need to have positive interactions—with people and with each other. If more shelters put that simple lesson into practice, I fervently believe we would have many more dogs that potential adopters would come to love.

Cats weren't much different. I opened all the cages in the cat room and let them interact in shifts, throughout the day.

I also began to make staff changes. I hired and trained my own people. I built a team, and then I began to focus on policies and procedures. Our animals now came through a process, from assessment to enrichment, and most were adopted within fewer than four weeks of their arrival in the shelter.

We also began to get out into the community with a free spay and neuter program, among other initiatives. And, in a sign that WARL was really turning around, we brought in more animals. Because we were actually adopting out animals, we created a program called ShARE—Shelter Animal Relief Effort—where we pulled animals from overcrowded municipal shelters and brought them to WARL. We set them up for success and were more likely to find them permanent, loving homes.

By 2004, three years into my tenure at WARL, we were operating efficiently and to the highest of standards; however, we were increasingly hampered by a building that desperately needed to catch up with its mission.

I assigned myself the task of conceptualizing and designing an animal shelter that truly would put animals first, designed from their perspective. I didn't know exactly how my vision would become reality, and I certainly didn't have all the answers. But the starting point to me couldn't have been clearer. Cages had to go.

I believed then, and still do today, that we must make the shelter's primary focus the animal and not the human visitor. By taking care of the animals, you create a thriving, positive environment. People will follow. People will respond—not only visitors and potential adopters, but staff members and volunteers as well.

To my base of practical knowledge, I added research. There were, at that time, relatively few scientific studies about animal sheltering, but there was considerable research about the human prison system and how design changes could reduce violence.

I formulated a plan, an articulated vision of what kind of a shelter I wanted to create. But that vision was sufficiently extreme that a board member whom I gave a preview to couldn't understand it. It needed to be more concrete, she told me. I had twenty-four board members to convince, and talk of a shelter without cages and with heated floors, elevated beds and perches, and water therapy systems just didn't compute. The board member urged me to meet with an architect and commit my plans to drawings. My only condition was that I would only work with an architect who had never designed—or, if possible, even stepped into—an animal shelter. I was not going to wind up with a new version of the same old things: lofty lobby, new steel bars, decorative tile walls, and dyed and sealed concrete floors. We were going to design a shelter for animals. I wound up working with an architect, Jeff Stoiber, who rapidly came to understand that I didn't care about human-style amenities inside an enclosure of steel bars. We had to do better.

Jeff also readily grasped the notion of "compassion fatigue." It's a buzzword that's been around for a couple of decades. What it really means is that when you put people into a depressing environment to do a difficult job, the job rapidly takes a toll on those workers. Of course, it isn't a concept limited to animal shelters—as more than a few nurses, personal caregivers, and special education teachers can attest. But in an animal shelter, if you create an environment where the animals can thrive, people who work or volunteer there are more likely to respond positively over a sustained period of time.

Because I was trying to do something so radical, there was no model to follow. Some organizations around the United States were doing innovative things, and I readily copied the best ideas. A shelter in Knoxville, Tennessee, for example, put steps in their puppy enclosures to help dogs develop their muscles by allowing them to climb and descend. The steps also allowed the pups to elevate themselves from their waste. A few shelters had already begun to house dogs and cats in glass rooms, but most of those were intended to be showcases in shelter lobbies for select animals. The large majority of animals were still being housed in traditional cages in the back of the shelter.

We borrowed and we innovated, and the result is still being copied today.

We created a room—a den, we called it—for each dog (or pair of compatible dogs). With steel bars and chain link out of the question, we made each den out of glass. The bottom three feet were constructed of translucent glass block, which allowed light to filter in but obscured the barrier-rage-inducing images of other dogs. Dogs could see movement through the blocks, giving the illusion of a greater world. The upper parts of the den were clear glass, which made it easy for staff members and potential adopters to see the dogs and for the dogs to see that abundant life still existed beyond the den. And that was just the beginning.

We realized early in the planning process that air in the shelter was no small matter. We put an independent air-supply vent and an air-exhaust vent in each den, with an air exchange rate that exceeded occupational safety requirements for human workplaces. That is important for comfort, yes, but also to significantly reduce the chances of spreading airborne pathogens. But for the air in each enclosure to be independently regulated, we needed to put some kind of a roof over each den. That design would be no small feat, but that process ultimately led to one of the shelter's crowning innovations.

Since we wanted each den to be filled with natural light, the roof would need to be made of glass. Why have those skylights if we didn't intend to take advantage of them? But in an animal shelter, a glass roof would quickly become dusty, dirty, and filter out the light, whether we liked it or not. The answer came to me through harp music.

In planning the shelter, I sought the opinions of dozens of experts from numerous disciplines and backgrounds. Some of them were holistic veterinarians. One, who was particularly enthused about the plans, noted that I planned to have a speaker in each dog room that would pipe in New Age music. Doing that was certainly not a musical preference. Studies suggested that New Age music created a calm, soothing environment for animals—and for people, too. The veterinarian asked if I had considered piping in harp music instead. It hadn't occurred to me and I asked why. "Because the harp simulates water," she said, handing me a study that backed up the harp-water association and the calming effects of the harp.

Once again, a light bulb went off: a gentle, soothing sound with positive, stimulating movement. That was how we would address the ceiling: with glass and water. We could make the roof of the dog den from one piece of glass, pitch it at a forty-five degree angle, and run a steady cascade of filtered and recycled water down the ceiling and into a collection trough over every dog den. Forget the calming simulation of water. We could use the real thing.

When I told some animal behavior specialists about the roof idea, they questioned whether the running water might be a problem for dogs afraid of storms. The truth was, I had no study to back up the idea. I had no proof, just a hunch coupled with the belief that dogs are smart enough to recognize the difference between a storm and calm, flowing water. I decided to take the chance.

The chance paid off. Our dogs responded only positively to running water—a very tranquil sound, indeed. Never did a dog mistake the tranquil water for a storm.

The dog dens also featured self-filling water bowls, which were plumbed from the bottom and just four inches wide. That meant no more mopping up after dogs that overturned their water bowls and simpler cleaning procedures. For the dogs it meant water that was more enticing because it was always fresh, circulating, and slightly aerated.

Another failure of the traditional shelter that we set out to remedy was a deceptively simple item: the door. More often than not, the door of a dog enclosure is made of chain link or steel bars and then plastered with signs: staff notes, intake paperwork, placards warning you to keep your fingers out, handwritten notes assessing the dog's behavior. The result is pure confusion, with one sign after the next, with no thought about what message the signs will convey to visitors. What you've actually created is yet another barrier.

I did away with signs. The glass door of the den was unadorned. Alongside the door of each dog's den was a card holder that contained printouts of basic information on the dog that visitors could take with them. It was just one more piece of negativity removed, replaced with valuable information.

And then there was the door itself. Our dog enclosures had Dutch doors. They were frosted on the bottom and clear on the top so visitors could look in, open the top half of the door, and interact with the dog. Rather than just staring at him, a visitor could touch the dog and get an inkling of his personality. If a dog wasn't ready for interaction, was sick, or if she was still in her assessment stage, the staff could lock the top of the door—a simple system that made it even easier to avoid a door covered by notes and signs. We accomplished something I had never seen before in a shelter. We linked the dog to human interaction at first sight.

Materials mattered, too. The floors were all a specialized acrylic material, with a drainage system in each enclosure. We covered the walls that were not glass with Corian brand material, which doesn't harbor bacteria and can be buffed periodically to retain its new look. We paid attention, as well, to colors. Dogs are apparently colorblind, so our color choices had little to do with their needs. But in the human prison system, studies indicate that earth tones and pastels are non-violent colors. I used those throughout, not for the potential benefit to dogs but certainly for the benefit of the staff and visitors. It was important, in our attention to detail, that we took care of the animals, staff, volunteers, and adopters. Above the door of each enclosure was a space for logos and acknowledgments of those who had purchased naming rights to help make this place of dignity a reality.

In most shelters, dog kennels back up to one another. Shelters workers can move a dog from one side to the other while cleaning. But the unused side of the kennel, when not being used for cleaning, would sit empty, thereby wasting half of the dog space. My dog dens also backed up to each other, but they led to a long alleyway in between. Each dog den had a vertically sliding "guillotine" door leading to the alley. The guillotine doors, made of heavy stainless steel, were connected at the front of the den to a counterweighted handle that allowed the door to open easily. Within seconds, we could have rows of dogs into the alleyway and out to the yard of the shelter, if there was ever a need to evacuate. We also made it possible to close off sections of the alleyway so we could have dogs in the alley space during cleaning, ultimately reclaiming 50 percent of the dog space and allowing us to shelter and serve many more dogs.

Although the dog area was a great deal larger, the cats at WARL got a fair shake at the new shelter. We built what we referred to as cat condos. They were double the size of the traditional steel cat cage. Cats were no longer forced to eliminate in the same area where they ate and slept. Each cat condo had its own litter box room. Oftentimes the more timid cats would use this room for security until they fully realized the safety of their temporary home. We included a perch above the litter box and a perch in the other area. Each condo was big enough to hold a cat bed, toys, and a scratching post. There were doors on either side that staff and volunteers could open to allow cats access from condo to condo, to meet their social needs.

Cats, too, had their own individual air exchanges, through the design we used in the dog dens. They had LED lighting inside of each room—daylight balanced and cool to the touch. One wall was glass block to allow daylight to penetrate. The cat room had music piped in.

We also made special playrooms for cats who didn't get along with others and acquaintance rooms for potential adopters to freely interact with the cats.

We incorporated the theme of water in the cat area, too. As most people who have cats are aware, they prefer oxygenated water. That's why, if your bathroom faucet has an aerator on the spigot, which mixes air and water, they jump up on the sink when you're brushing your teeth. To satisfy that desire, we created a large water tower for the cats with perches, so they could jump up and take a drink of aerated water or play with the water.

I didn't design the dog dens and cat condos to be cute but, again, to change attitudes. Most people—most animal adopters—don't think about the damage a cage does. That was my job.

But there was one label I wasn't willing to change: animal shelter. We faced some pressure to call ourselves an adoption center or community center. We had worked hard to create a new kind of animal shelter, and I wanted to change the stereotype, so people would think of a shelter as a place where we would care for the formerly discarded, where we would protect animals and allow compassion to blossom.

The day we moved the dogs and cats into the new, permanent space was an emotional one for everyone. I spent much of that day fighting back tears and some of it allowing them to flow. I had convinced twenty-four board members that I knew what I was doing, and they committed to a $6 million capital campaign for something that had never before been done. It worked. After we opened the new shelter on October 20, 2006, adoptions quadrupled.

The reviews were universally positive. *The Washington Post* published a photo essay titled "Peace at the Pound." An article in *USA Today* said, "Life is serene for the 270 homeless dogs and cats lounging about the adoption areas of the Washington Animal Rescue League, a recently renovated animal shelter that has spurned convention by elevating the temporary care, housing and rehabilitation of rejected pets to an entirely new level."

While that kind of free publicity was most welcome, I found I valued the personal interactions that were part of the day-to-day work even more. A couple of months into operation of the new shelter, on a Saturday, a visitor introduced himself. He looked familiar. "Didn't you just adopt here?" I asked.

"Yeah," he said. "We adopted a couple of weeks ago."

"Are you looking at another dog?"

"No, I just bring my kids here because it's a good, positive environment for them on the weekends."

I had a few conversations like that, each of which could not have made me happier. We had taken a facility that exemplified the stereotype of a dark, dingy, dirty place where animals expired or were put to death, and we turned it into a community animal shelter that exemplified the human-animal bond. Rather than going to the zoo or to the movies with their children, people were coming to WARL to embrace their compassion. Members of the community no longer looked away; they were adopting these soon-to-be companion animals.

We also made WARL a place of humane education. We had a safe environment where we could bring in kids from area schools, children whose only experiences with animals were often with pit bulls on chains or feral cats in alleys. These children had never heard a cat purr. They had never felt the joys of the soft fur from the chest of a dog or watched a puppy sleep. We brought in school kids to learn about animals in a safe, happy environment. For many of them, it was the first positive experience ever with an animal. Our hope was that it wasn't the last positive experience—that a spark of compassion could grow into a fire. Our shelter had a community room for meetings, classes, and even kids' birthday parties. It became a catalyst for compassion.

CHAPTER SIX

KATRINA

At two o'clock in the morning on September 12, 2005, a police officer pulled us over in New Orleans. I assumed he would order my colleagues and me out of town or ask for our credentials since it was past curfew. It turned out the only reason he was interested in us had to do with the Washington Animal Rescue League lettering and logo on the vehicle's side. He had never heard of WARL, but clearly the words "animal" and "rescue" had grabbed him. The officer told me he had been working around the clock for the not-quite two weeks since Hurricane Katrina hit New Orleans. He had gotten his kids and wife safely out of their home on the city's east side and out of the storm's path before it made landfall, but he had not been able to evacuate his three dogs. With emotion in his voice concerning their fate, he asked us to go check on the dogs. Despite the hour and our concerns that we wouldn't be able to get into his house because of high water levels, we headed that way.

We parked as close to the house as we could and then headed out on foot in dry suits to protect us from the toxic flood waters for the dozen blocks still to go. With each passing stretch of the neighborhood, the water became higher and higher. By the time we got close to his house, it was up to our chests.

Because of the depth of the flood we had to enter the house on the second floor and work our way down, as conditions would allow. We broke a window and climbed in. As we searched from room to room, illuminated only by our flashlights, I quickly caught sight of the body of one dog as it floated by. I knew at that moment that the other two had to have drowned or perished and ended up in the water. Moments later, I found what I was expecting: the body of a second dog. Then I heard a noise coming from another room. It was quite spooky; the noise made no sense. Nothing was moving, and no one was alive. I pushed the door open, which was no small feat, given the water and mud. I began to sweep my flashlight across the room that had fallen silent. Perhaps the water had caused two items in the room to rub against each other. There were plenty of possible explanations and no time to contemplate them. And then my flashlight hit something that sparkled in the light. Sweeping the beam of light back to that point, I saw the body of the third dog. He had been standing on a windowsill, a ledge barely two inches deep, and he appeared to be frozen in place. But he was alive, and, in the end, elated to see us. We got him to the van and offered him some much-appreciated food and water. We reunited that dog with his guardian, a man who had, without any hesitation, put his community's needs in front of his own. It was a great honor. It was one person, one dog, and one case out of hundreds I faced in New Orleans, but it is one that will always stand out.

An estimated 25,000 animals perished in Hurricane Katrina and its aftermath. No one knows how many thousands more were left without shelter or abandoned by residents who were not allowed to take their companion animals with them when they evacuated.

Professional animal rescue teams had traveled *en masse* to New Orleans, responding to a call from the Humane Society of the United States to contribute resources to this urgent need. I had been trained under a program of theirs called NDART: National Disaster Animal Rescue Team. The NDART training, which I would later work to reinvent, was modeled after a curriculum of the Federal Emergency Management Agency. Little of its training pertained to animals. But NDART was a national program, and it was a useful tool HSUS could use to reach groups that might be of help and to organize the animal welfare response to Katrina, as well as other natural disasters and emergency situations.

As soon as the call went out, we mobilized a team from WARL.

The first task for the animal rescue effort was to figure out how to get access to the city. FEMA hadn't yet allowed animal groups into New Orleans. In natural disasters, animal groups have to be invited in and sanctioned by state, county, or local officials—or, in some cases, a local humane society—before they can provide any assistance. In the days immediately after the levees broke in New Orleans, the only community that had approved having animal groups come in was Slidell, a small city on the northeast side of Lake Pontchartrain, across from New Orleans. A group there had set up an emergency shelter. They weren't organizing rescues but were receiving animals. In response to a call for veterinarians, we sent down Dr. Gary Weitzman from WARL, who helped organize the first triage unit for animals affected by Katrina.

When we first pulled up to a checkpoint in New Orleans, we passed a row of cars lined up on the side of the road, with people standing outside their vehicles. At the time, only emergency responders were being allowed into the city, and those permissions now extended to animal responders. The people outside their cars watched us closely as we slowly drove past. Just as we were about to reach the checkpoint, after they saw the WARL lettering on the side of our van, some of those people rushed toward us. Through the windows, we were bombarded with folded pieces of paper. Inside each was a key. Written on each paper was a name, an address, a cell phone number if they had one, and a description of the animal or animals trapped in their houses. Some people got on their knees, with tears streaming down their faces, begging us to rescue their animals. At that point, I knew we were about to enter what was uncharted territory.

As soon as we entered the city, it became obvious we were in the midst of a catastrophe that defied description.

We already had with us a set of marching orders: our assigned territory, addresses, and animals—information that had been reported to the call center. But block by block, more passersby, and even National Guard members, flagged us down about still more missing animals. We hadn't yet rescued one animal, and we were drastically behind.

The emergency shelter we were assigned to, the place that was supposed to receive our rescued animals and that we would call home base, was in the Lamar-Dixon Expo Center, a large equine center in Gonzales, about an hour northwest of New Orleans, half-way to Baton Rouge. For sleeping accommodations, each animal rescuer was assigned a patch of lawn. When I was able to sleep, when I could put out of my head every situation I hadn't yet been able to resolve, my resting spot was on a tree root.

Over the next six weeks, we never caught up with the demand. We would come to an address that was next on our list and res-cue the dog or cat trapped in the water-logged house. But while we were there, we would hear more animals—next door, down the block, up the street, or around the corner. We would park our van in one spot and, within thirty minutes, it was full. A mission designed to find one dog or cat would yield twenty or more. There were more animals than we could rescue. Governed almost entirely by sheer logistics, I had to pick and choose whose life I was going to save that day. There were animals on rooftops, animals trapped in houses, and animals on land. The priority became the ones trapped in houses. We knew the temperatures inside were high, that the air was stale, and that most animals were still contending with flood water. The animals on the street were at least a little better able to fend off the elements because they were mobile. The ones on rooftops were, as long as they stayed in place, not in danger of drowning.

We would load the van in no time at all. We made several trips to the emergency shelter each eighteen- to twenty-hour day. There were plenty of obstacles. Some of them were entirely bureaucratic.

One of the first nights, we returned to the emergency shelter about nine o'clock and joined a small but growing line of vehicles, all full of rescued animals. One dog had already died in my van that day. The gates were closed. A security guard wouldn't let any of us in. I got out of my vehicle, walked down the fence until I found a low spot, climbed over, and went looking for the person in charge. The best I could locate was the person who had sent us out into the field earlier in the day.

"What's going on?" I asked her with more than a little annoyance in my voice. "You've got vehicles backed up out there, vehicles full of animals needing veterinary care."

"The state has put a stop on how many animals can be in the emergency shelter," she replied. We have 2,000 animals and they're not going to allow any more."

"OK," I replied. "But you have a problem right now. You sent dozens of vehicles out to rescue animals today and we're all backed up at the fucking gate and we've got no place to go."

By now, the line of vehicles stretched a good quarter mile.

"We're working on it," she said.

"What do you mean, you're working on it? You're not even communicating anything to anybody."

"I'll send someone out there to communicate that we're working on it."

A person standing nearby volunteered to do the job. But she knew nothing. Everyone was frustrated. We were exhausted and the animals who were sick and injured and had been starving, thirsty, and frightened for days were sitting in cages, in vehicle after vehicle.

Meanwhile, the emergency shelter staff, finally working with more urgency, searched for a solution. They contacted an evacuation shelter at Louisiana State University in Baton Rouge—a facility that was housing animals that were evacuated before the storm— but it was not accepting unclaimed animals. That shelter relented, though, just for that one night. They agreed to bend the rules and take all of the animals from all of the vehicles—with one caveat: no pit bulls. And that was all that I had. Several other vehicles were in the same situation.

After I protested, a woman from the ASPCA made more calls and, she said, persuaded the evacuation shelter to give special permission to accept pit bulls for that one night.

So off our caravan went to Baton Rouge. We waited in line. After two hours, when my turn came, I was told they weren't going to accept pit bulls. I argued my case, as strenuously as you might imagine, to no avail.

I called back to the original emergency shelter. "I've got a truck full of pit bulls, and, despite the assurances you were given, they're not taking my animals. What do I do?"

"I don't know."

"Let me talk to the person in charge."

"He's sleeping." It was now after midnight.

"Well, wake him up."

Finally, somebody went to get the man. "I'm sorry," he said. "I don't know what to tell you."

"You told me to go out and rescue animals. I did. You sent me all over the place. You're wasting my time, and now you tell me you have no plan for my pit bulls?"

"Yeah," he answered. He was as stuck as I was, but didn't share my responsibility and commitment to these specific animals.

I was left with a problem I had to take care of for myself.

I called the facility in Slidell where Gary Weitzman was working and talked to the person in charge. She agreed to take the estimated fifty pit bulls we had in several vehicles.

The trip would have been relatively simple—were Interstate 10 intact. Instead, the trip took three hours. We pulled in, dispirited and girded for rejection yet again, but were greeted by an army of compassionate people who took the dogs and took care of us. One of my team members was experiencing symptoms of lupus. The shelter had a medical person standing by to take care of her.

In New Orleans, the dangers were numerous and the opportunities for adequate personal hygiene were lacking. The waters in the streets of New Orleans contained cars, boats, snakes, and more than a few alligators. All of us were one slip and fall away from an injury that could turn nasty. We had infections and rashes. I first took a shower on day ten, with chlorinated water from the back of a truck.

As in any crisis, the Katrina rescue effort was full of rumors, many of which were reported in the media. My wife would continually update me with things she had heard, out of concern for my welfare. As I was driving through the city, she called to pass along a report that aircraft would soon move across New Orleans, dropping pesticides, and that officials had ordered people out. As I was listening on the speakerphone, trying to calculate how much time I had to drive out of danger, I heard the sound of aircraft and, moments later, had a load of pesticides spread all over our van.

We also developed what we called "Katrina cough." The floodwaters brought in mud and muck, which became infused with various toxins. As that water receded, the muck dried and became a fine dust we all breathed. Within days, we all developed a rasp. You could tell if someone was freshly arrived just by hearing his unaffected voice.

Because of the inefficiencies and bureaucratic hurdles of the emergency sheltering system, I often found myself having to devise my own solutions, to create my own efficiencies. When I would hear or see an animal and then forcibly enter a house to rescue him, it wouldn't take long to find a piece of paper—a utility bill or a letter—that would contain a phone number and eventually lead me—sometimes after four or five phone calls—to the resident of that home. I was able to talk to the guardian of the animal I was rescuing, in many cases, immediately after I located the animal. Not only was I rescuing the family's companion animal, I was almost always the first person to give that person an eyewitness account of what she had lost, what the property looked like. I was a lifeline.

Most assumed their houses were total losses. It was a privilege to be there for these families, and I took that part of my job as seriously as any.

Eventually, there were receiving centers inside the city, where we could drop off animals who would then be transported by tractor-trailer to the emergency shelters. Without those long drives back and forth, the pace of rescues picked up considerably. But even with those receiving centers in place, I still tried, whenever possible, to avoid the system altogether. If I was able to reach an animal's companion after making a rescue, I tried to arrange a direct return, taking the shelter out of the equation entirely. When I would call a resident, I would identify myself as an animal rescuer "and I am in your house." The reactions ranged from "Is he alive?" to "How is my house?" to "We left him behind. We have no interest in reclaiming him." In some cases, when a companion relinquished animals to me, I found volunteers to house them until I could send a van-full back to WARL.

Four hundred people from New Orleans were evacuated to Washington, DC, following Katrina. Most were housed in the D.C. Armory, a massive building right next to the Robert F. Kennedy Memorial Stadium. Two of those people had gone on the television news in Washington, telling stories of lost animals. My staff at WARL told me their stories and urged me to find those animals. With some deft detective work, we found them and brought them back with us to D.C. in a van full of animals. We reunited a man named Wayne Mancuso and his two cats, Simba and Dargee.

A local television station was there to capture the moment. Holding Simba as he sat in the WARL veterinary office, his voice choked with emotion, Wayne said, "To be reunited is the greatest thing in the world." Wayne eventually moved back to New Orleans. He passed away a year later. One of his dying wishes was that the cats would be returned to WARL and adopted out to a new family. We went and got them, and then we found the pair a home—together.

We saw a lot of death—animal and human—and saved a lot of lives after Katrina. But after six weeks, I needed to get back to Washington to tend to my shelter. I had a fundraiser I needed to attend to help defray the costs of our operations in New Orleans. The idea was that I would jump off the plane, put on a suit, tell some stories of triumph and tragedy, and raise a lot of money. That didn't happen.

When I boarded the plane and sat still for a few minutes, I found myself overcome by everything I had just experienced. I broke down. I was suddenly unable to control the emotions I had put aside for six weeks. The next thing I knew, I was in a cab in D.C., on the way to a hotel for the fundraiser. As soon as I got there, I grabbed members of my board of directors, broke down again in front of them, and told them I couldn't speak. The event went on, but I was never on the podium. In the days that followed, I saw a counselor who specialized in compassion fatigue, and I mandated that my field team from New Orleans do the same.

I was home for about a week, trying to unwind and decompress and spend some quality time with my wife and kids. But even when I was home, part of me was still in New Orleans. The situation had gripped me, and I couldn't let go. I particularly couldn't let go of the image of a small white dog trapped under the crumpled remains of a house. We spent hours taking the house off of the dog. We got him. He died an hour later.

I headed back to New Orleans and continued to provide more resources for the community. WARL became a resource for overwhelmed shelters trying to persevere.

Katrina reminded us that, in dealing with natural disasters, prevention is always the best method. In the fall of 2006, President Bush signed into law the Pets Evacuation and Transportation Standards Act (PETS), which required that, in disasters, states address the needs of companion animals through evacuation and co-habitated evacuation shelters, with FEMA footing the bill and reimbursing states and counties for work to rescue, shelter, and care for animals.

I was in charge of HSUS responses in 2008, as its senior director of emergency services, when Hurricane Gustav hit, bearing down yet again on New Orleans. Animal organizations moved in and took animals to Shreveport, where they received care, in close proximity to where their human companions had been evacuated.

Today, I make myself available to talk to local organizations tasked with emergency preparations for companion animals, whether in human-caused or natural disasters. Once a disaster hits, things can get complicated in a hurry. Neighboring jurisdictions must have memoranda of understanding in place so they can cooperate in the protection of animals. Bureaucracies rapidly get in the way of common sense. Plans and preparations in the United States have improved since Katrina, but how well they have improved is still a question. It will take the next major Katrina-sized disaster for us to find out.

In late August of 2007, two WARL vans again made the sixteen-hour drive to New Orleans, arriving just in time to mark the second anniversary of Hurricane Katrina. I preceded them by a couple of days, accompanied by Rich, my co-author. The trip allowed me to see how New Orleans and its animals were recovering.

My team and I traveled to New Orleans at its most stiflingly hot and humid time of year on a mission that went beyond marking an anniversary. We planned to fill up our vans with animals from overloaded shelters and get them to WARL for assessment, rehabilitation, and adoption. We could have used an entire fleet of vans, but we managed with the two we had.

One shelter I visited, about sixty miles outside of New Orleans, was depressingly typical. It was concrete and cages. There were outside runs full of dogs. The inside kennels, with only fans to ventilate them, weren't much better. We saw portable dog cages stacked three high in any available space. "We stay full every day," said an attendant, in a video Rich shot. Dressed in medical scrubs and clearly eager to tell someone her story, she continued, in heartbreaking detail. "We do euthanasia every single day, fifty to sixty animals a day, because we have no space…. One day I had to eutha-nize sixty-three animals, which ripped my heart out." We intended to change that, if only temporarily.

We had to quickly assess and count animals and conditions, because I intended to fill those two vans with every dog or cat I could. The clouds were turning ominous as a thunderstorm approached. But on that one day in that one shelter, no animals were put to death. We took them all, along with a number of other animals that friends of WARL had asked us to rescue.

One of the dogs we were fortunate to bring back was a hound mix named Sweetie. The shelter had heard reports she was liv-ing along a rural highway, but despite repeated sightings, no one had attempted to bring her in. A brown, black, and white girl with floppy ears and gentle disposition, Sweetie was pregnant when a volunteer finally brought her to the shelter. Sweetie's puppies had been adopted, but she remained, probably because of her right front leg, which appeared to have been badly broken at some point. Her paw was severely curled under. She walked—slowly and unstead-ily—on her wrist. Sweetie had been fostered by a couple named Eric and Brenda. It was obvious that they cared deeply for her, but they lacked the means to get her the care and rehabilitation she needed. We all cried when a member of my crew placed her gin-gerly into one of the vans. I hugged Eric and Brenda, and thanked them for their compassion. I promised them that their good deeds in caring for her would be matched by the care my staff at WARL would offer her.

The trip back to Washington—each van piloted by a team of two—was a long, mad dash. The teams were transporting pup-pies and adult dogs, large dogs and small dogs, and a bunch of cats. Like most any animal transport for a rescue group, the teams drove straight through, stopping only to get gas and quickly allow the animals to relieve themselves and get a bit of exercise—always keeping the vans' air conditioners set to their most frigid. After twenty hours on the road, the two vans pulled up in front of WARL, greeted by cheers and tears. Sweetie—who became known at WARL as Sweets—received all of the care she needed and wound up, like all the others we brought back, in a permanent, loving home.

Some might call that mission a small gesture, but I disagree. More than one hundred lives saved is neither small, nor a gesture.

CHAPTER SEVEN

MY COMPANION ANIMAL FAMILY

While I have led the rescues of more than a quarter million animals, very few have made it into my home. During my first stint at the Washington Humane Society, I fell in love for the first time.

He was chained in a backyard, emaciated and almost dead, a Rottweiler probably just under a year old. I saw a familiar vacancy in his eyes. He was done. They were eyes that were finished with suffering. They were eyes that had succumbed to death. But in the moment our eyes met, as I lifted him from the neglect of his life, I saw—or at least believed I saw—a glimmer. Did we really connect? I don't know. Did I feel a connection? Absolutely. I adopted Capone and took him home.

Al Capone is one of America's most storied gangsters. His activities during the Prohibition era were a laundry list of vices and crimes. But Capone also sponsored one of the country's first soup kitchens during the Great Depression. He was an utterly contradictory mix of gangster, killer, bootlegger, and humanitarian. He was feared and beloved. He is a significant part of American history. The canine Capone was fearsome to the eye, but remarkably sweet and gentle, despite the life he came from.

I nursed Capone back to health, slowly getting him back to his normal weight. We went on hikes along the Potomac River and long walks in my Adams Morgan neighborhood of Washington, DC. Everywhere we went, it seemed, people who got to know Capone loved him. We would walk along 18th Street, past rows of bars and clubs. More than a few owners would see Capone coming and run out to offer him a treat. I actually had to sidestep certain restaurants to avoid the digestive concerns that would follow Capone's ingestion of too much of certain kinds of people food.

One unforgettable night, when we were on a walk in our neighborhood. Capone was off leash but not far away. We were strolling through a schoolyard; the area was minimally lit, and Capone was darker still. He trotted off somewhere to do his business. I kept walking, knowing he wouldn't venture far and would come to me if I called his name. I didn't notice other people just ahead of me: two guys lurking, waiting for someone to come through. They jumped out, from opposites sides, and headed straight toward me. I never saw their faces, and they didn't speak, but it was clear that they were converging on me, and not to have a friendly conversation. I was about to be robbed and probably get my ass kicked, too. In the second or two it took me to realize the gravity of the situation, I grunted just one word through my clenched teeth: "Capone!" He responded immediately, trotting toward me. He wasn't barking, wasn't growling, and didn't have teeth bared. He was just returning to me. But my attackers didn't know that. He was big, intimidating, and a Rottweiler. The two went flying in opposite directions. It was the sight of Capone that kept me intact that night.

Capone was my best friend. He taught me about companionship and about the responsibilities of caring for him. He was smart, and we developed a bond the likes of which I had never known before. But that bond became much more.

I still find it difficult to explain, but Capone became my everything. He was my life. He was my first love. He was my muse. And he was also my filter. I processed everything through Capone.

Capone came into my life at a time when I was continually learning. Getting an education and working with animals had opened up new horizons. I was absorbing issues about animals and developing my way of thinking about issues surrounding animal protection. In virtually every situation I encountered with animals, I used Capone as my example, my filter through which I viewed what was in front of me. When I rescued an animal, I would think about what I would want for Capone. When I looked at a primate in a cage, a chicken in a farmhouse, or a mink being injected in his stomach with toxins that would kill him but preserve his fur, I saw Capone. Virtually every time I made a decision, I projected it through Capone. Capone was my inspiration to provide animals the highest level of care I was equipped to provide. He reminded me that I had been given a tremendous responsibility—to help rewrite the destiny of abused, unwanted animals. As I progressed in my rescue work, he was the driving force.

Capone moved with me to New York City and to San Francisco. When I made the move to the Bay Area, I had a girlfriend who accompanied me. We drove a large Ryder rental truck with four seats in the cab. Behind the driver and passenger seats, a pair of jump seats faced each other. I fitted a piece of plywood to bridge the seats and make a bed for Capone. With a soft futon mattress on top, he got to ride in style. He was up high in the cab. He could see the road, and he could see us.

When I moved back to Washington, this time by myself, he was right there on his special seat in a different truck, but still cruising in style.

Capone was also the reason I came to share my life and home with cats. I lived then in an art studio loft on Capitol Hill. I worked long hours, but I would break away to take him on walks. Still, I felt bad that Capone didn't have companionship when I was away. I decided to get another animal. I had fostered a number of dogs and had witnessed his apparent unease at sharing me with another. So I decided to get a cat. I had always had a particular attraction to gray cats and orange tabbies. I began looking.

One day not long after, I got a call about a stray cat on an apartment balcony. It was a fairly common call, to come get a cat that had "just shown up." But four stories up on an apartment balcony? It was suspicious. Imagine, then, my surprise when the stray story seemed to be true. The apartment dweller genuinely seemed not to know the cat—a kitten, actually—who, she said, had been lying on his back sunning himself all day. I guessed the cat to be about two months old. I went out to get him, prepared for the cat to panic and jump from the balcony. The cat I encountered purred at me and sought affection. I hadn't really noticed until then that he was gray.

Most of the time, a stray animal coming into a shelter doesn't have a name but once in a while, when a name just seemed to fit, I added one to his paperwork. When I got this cat to the shelter I named him "Neo," after the hero in the film *The Matrix*. Neo is also an anagram of "one," which, according to the movie, is a sign of his destiny to be "The One."

I went to visit Neo in the shelter the next day before my shift, a frequent practice of mine, to check on animals I had brought in, to see how they were adjusting, and to find out if they had any adoptions pending. I got to the cat room and found Neo sharing his cage with a cat that could have been a carbon copy. She had been surrendered to the shelter, and the cat supervisor found her compatible with Neo, whom she pushed me to adopt. And then, being a true cat person, she pushed me further, to adopt both cats. It worked. I named her Bleu.

Neo had the mannerisms and temperament of a dog. Bleu was more feline and independent. But Capone proved perfectly compatible with both of them. Neo died of cancer in 2008. Bleu is still with us, at the ripe age of seventeen. For a long time she gravitated toward men, but over the years she has become, for all intents and purposes, my daughters' cat.

When I got married, Capone shared his life with my wife and her two dogs. Capone died June 4, 2003, just three months before the birth of our first child.

I had seen a lot of death and trauma, but Capone's passing was the most difficult thing I had ever been through. He died lying next to me, at home, with an intravenous line in his leg providing essential fluids. I had never dealt with losing a loved one, and it was a long process. Capone had collapsed three or four times over the last two years of his life. Each time I thought it might be the end. I didn't want him to suffer; I was prepared to euthanize him. But each of those times, he bounced back. That made his death all that much harder.

I knew he was suffering. But I didn't know he was dying the last time he collapsed. I thought he might come back once more. Watching him suffer was horrible. I did everything I could to give him comfort. On his last night, we were cuddled close to each other. I woke up in the same spot the next morning. He was in the same spot, too. He died while we slept.

I felt grief for sure, but I was also greatly upset with myself, because I knew he had suffered, and I didn't alleviate that suffering for him. While we certainly communicated with each other, Capone couldn't tell me that he was near death. He had always come back. Had I known, I would have opted for euthanasia, to end his pain.

Some people talk to their dogs; they have one-sided conversations. I didn't talk to Capone; I didn't pour my heart out to him. I didn't need to. The bond was so strong there was no need to communicate verbally. We knew what to do together. We knew what one another's needs were. The end of his life was the exception.

If I could have one wish, it would be to spend five minutes in the head of Capone, to see the world he saw, to understand his world, if only to make me better at what I do, to be better at serving animals.

But I wanted him back. I spent time looking for another Capone. I was focused on a Rottweiler and looked at twenty or so, in rescue environments. It made me realize how fortunate I was to get a Rottweiler with such a mild temperament, who was kind to everybody. I went to shelters in New York, Philadelphia, Pittsburgh, Atlanta, and all over the Washington area. I was going everywhere looking for a Rottweiler—or mixed breed—in a rescue environment that was everything Capone was. I couldn't find that dog.

My search for the ideal dog coincided with an initiative at WARL to take in animals from overcrowded municipal shelters. Our first such partners were from the city of Baltimore and Prince George's County in Maryland. Because of the success of these programs, we began looking for placement partners in a wider area. One night I came across a dog on the Petfinder website who piqued my interest. A mix of a Chow Chow and a bloodhound, he was red, about eighty-five pounds, with a hound-like face that made him appear perpetually sad. I approached the Georgia facility that was housing him, expressed interest on behalf of WARL in making that shelter a placement partner, and headed south with our transport team. The facility was a long room with dogs in four-foot by four-foot cages. The cages were made of prison-like iron bars, which had been painted long enough ago that rust was taking over. The floors were crisscrossed steel grates, through which the dogs' waste could fall.

On our first meeting, neither the dog nor I felt what I was hoping for. He was almost a statue. He was defeated. He expressed no interest in me. As I walked him out, I said to my team, "This is Satchmo. He's got the blues."

People who knew Satchmo continually told me what a great dog he was, but I still didn't feel the emotion of a budding relationship. Satchmo would come back with us to WARL in any event, and we would find him a forever home, but I began to doubt that he and I were a match. Then my wife spoke. In a phone call home, she said, "He may not be the dog you expected him to be, but he was the dog you went to get. I think we should give him a chance." I have never been so grateful for her counsel. I grew to love Satchmo deeply, and he was my wife's all-time favorite dog. Their connection was special. Satchmo died March 17, 2015 at the age of fourteen, after losing his battle with cancer.

Then came a Greater Swiss Mountain Dog named Bergh.

Henry Bergh founded the American Society for the Prevention of Cruelty to Animals in 1866. Bergh was an aristocrat who had served as an American diplomat before he became an animal advocate known as The Great Meddler. He is one of my heroes. Bergh once summed up his life and work in a letter to a reporter: "Day after day I am in slaughterhouses, or lying in wait at midnight with a squad of police near some dog pit. Lifting a fallen horse to his feet, penetrating buildings where I inspect collars and saddles for raw flesh, then lecturing in public schools to children, and again to adult societies. Thus my whole life is spent."

The canine Bergh, who was about three years old, came from a puppy mill and was one of a dozen Swiss Mountain Dogs from a rescue I led while at WARL. In fact, they were among the first group of dogs to reside in the renovated shelter's glass-enclosed dens. The puppy mill operator told authorities that her dog trainer's methods included hitting dogs on the head with a frying pan. Bergh was housed in a building with no electricity and very little light, in a cinder block cell. Others would come and go, but Bergh was there for years on end. He was terrified of storms. He was abused and traumatized. He came to trust us, but he was always wary of the world. Bergh again became more of my wife's dog. She loved walking the huge, gorgeous, tri-colored dog and getting peoples' reactions.

Bergh developed a persistent cough while I was on a rescue operation in Canada. My wife took him to the vet. "He won't be leaving the clinic," she told me by phone. I drove straight back in record-breaking time and met her, my daughters, and my son at the veterinarian's office. The vet showed me the X-rays. He was riddled with cancer. We made the decision to euthanize him right then and there, a loss that deeply affected all of my family.

Animal Rescue Corps was part of the response to Hurricane Isaac in New Orleans in 2012. We took a team down to assist with recovery efforts and help a damaged shelter. We took dozens of dogs out and drove them to our emergency shelter in Tennessee, where we began placing dogs with various shelters and rescue groups. Eighteen were headed to rescue partners in Canada. But the last dog, a Great Pyreneese, would fit on the transport vehicle only if we removed three others. It made more sense to keep only one dog behind, to take her to Canada later, and I chose to foster her in the meantime.

I had identified a small mass on her chest, and by the time I got back to my home with her, there was no question it had grown. I took her to the vet, who confirmed the mass was cancer. The emaciated dog also had heartworm. The question was whether to treat the heartworm or the cancer first. The vet removed the mass and then, after several months, began treating the heartworm. By now, she was our dog, Magnolia, and my kids certainly weren't going to let me send her to Canada. Magnolia also happened to be one of the sweetest dogs I ever met. Two years later, she developed a secondary cancer. This time it was inoperable, in the chest and foreleg. Our objective was simply to keep her comfortable. The vet euthanized her at home. Watching my kids say goodbye was almost as difficult as the loss. I have brought my kids on transports with rescued dogs, and as a result they have a deeper knowledge than the average kid about cruelty and our society's exploitation of animals. But Magnolia's death was about pure, and raw, emotion.

Thinking back on all of the animals that have lived in my home, my thoughts and some of my fondest memories go back to Capone, to the relationship that was like no other. I think about the privilege of taking care of Capone during his final days. It was an honor to know him and to be with him at his end, trying to convey to him that he had nothing to worry about.

Despite my love and affection for Capone and all the other animals who have followed, I am conflicted by the idea of having a companion animal. I don't believe I have the right to possess another living being. As I see it, I rescue them. I am their provider, guardian, caretaker, and servant, because they don't have any other option since we humans domesticated them. Most of us in the animal protection field were inspired by the bonds we have with our companion animals. It starts there in most cases. In that respect, I am grateful for that bond. Capone enhanced my life and my career, and I'm damn glad of it. But I believe that of the animals society calls companion animals, most of those who are abused or neglected suffer that mistreatment while living in a home. I would just as soon we not have companion animals at all, if setting them free could end suffering. It doesn't matter, of course, because that is unrealistic. But I wish more people would see the family companion animal as something other than the lowest rung in that family. Compassion should have no boundaries or hierarchy. Animals make us better people. Rescuing them isn't a one-way street.

CHAPTER EIGHT

A BROADER REACH

My goal continues to be abolishing cages and breaking chains, both physical and metaphorical. I have a deep respect for all life—all beings. As I mentioned earlier, at the time I was considering entering the field of animal protection, I also gave considerable thought to the field of child protection. I could see myself investigating cases of child abduction and the international trafficking of children. I mention that to make the point yet again that I do not differentiate between levels of lives. I don't believe we have to choose between the protection of animals and the protection of children. There should be enough compassion among us to make humane choices for all. I am often asked why I put so much effort into animals when I could help people. This question arises from a hierarchical view of the world. I set high standards for the protection and care of animals because their lives deserve respect and justice. In just the same manner, if I ran a homeless shelter or human protection organization, it would have the highest standards of care.

At WARL I conceived of a shelter that established a new standard in animal care, which rapidly became a model that other communities and rescue organizations studied and sometimes emulated. From that vantage point, I found it a good time to look back, to contemplate my journey so far, and consider next steps— for me, of course, but also for the cause of animal protection. We had demonstrated, with WARL, that one shelter, driven by compassion, high standards, and humane philosophies, could affect a city. But how, I asked myself, do you change a country?

It had now been more than fifteen years since I became an animal control officer. I had worked on more than a few cases of large-scale animal suffering. I had come to appreciate every opportunity to be a leader in order to end suffering. I appreciated the chance to share my compassion with like-minded people—and even to convey my inspiration with people who weren't necessarily like-minded. My life's experiences and my street smarts had given me the capacity and ability to push through things, to adapt to almost any situation. I have spoken to drug addicts, using my story to assist them in changing their lives. I have spoken to businesspeople, striving to impart some creative thinking and strategies they could apply to their work. I have spoken to children, some who were in school and some who were already in trouble. I speak to donors, who share my compassion, because they believe in my work and want to support my cause.

Despite some of the hardships I have experienced throughout my years, I maintain a positive outlook on life. I am not fond of complainers, people who use the words "can't," "don't," "won't," or "impossible." If you use those kinds of defeatist words with me, I won't argue with you. More than likely, I go vacant. We all have moments when we don't know if we can accomplish a task in front of us. Doubts are fine. I can help you overcome them. But I don't have any appreciation for people who feel sorry for themselves and who choose defeat without even trying.

While I contemplated what would come next, I had one of my last victories at WARL. We cared for the Michael Vick dogs. The professional football quarterback and several associates had been charged by federal authorities with animal abuse and dogfighting. Vick was alleged to have been directly involved in the operation, including the brutal execution of dogs. Officials had seized dozens of pit bulls.

I received a call one day from a federal official who was tasked with the dogs' care during the judicial process. She had recently read a media story about the new WARL, and she asked me if I would take on the eleven dogs who were most mentally and physically damaged. They remained, at that time, in a shelter in rural Virginia, not far from the farm where they had been housed and abused. She asked me to assume responsibility for their care, recovery, and enrichment until the conclusion of the trial. Of course, I said yes.

Before I could take custody of the dogs, we had to modify the facility in order to keep the dogs in a secure, private area, and I needed to appoint a principal caretaker. Attorneys were involved to draft a memorandum of understanding, which included the condition that I not divulge beyond key staff members the origin or identities of the dogs. To meet the need for security, I took one row of the dog room and had floor-to-ceiling plywood walls constructed. No one could see into the area. We had only twenty-four hours to prepare. I brought in two additional caretakers and a trainer, who put together an enrichment plan. My only condition for the authorities was that I receive permission to spay and neuter the dogs and perform any necessary medical procedures and treatments. They made that happen.

Once I had the authority to get the dogs, I wasn't going to waste any time, under any circumstances. I sent two members of my staff to get them. Had the dogs not already been in dire straits, the team reported, they would have been if they'd stayed much longer at this rural pound. They found a filthy facility, with feces and urine everywhere, and more than one dead dog in a cage, more than likely having succumbed to Parvo.

The dogs arrived late in the evening, and they were as anyone would expect: frightened dogs in transition. They were nervous and uncertain, physically and spiritually broken. They all had very visible scars. Several had their teeth filed down. One had a broken jaw. They were broken dogs, but other than their notoriety, they were much like thousands of dogs I had seen before. The most tragic stories were of the dogs we were too late to help—dogs Vick owned that were electrocuted, beaten with a baseball bat, hanged, and thrown against walls.

The reward for us was to watch these abused creatures turn into dogs. We worked to assess them and understand their issues. We watched them trust us, trust one another, and trust other dogs. We offered them high-value treats and other enrichment items. It all started with a clean environment that met their basic needs. They were all individuals, and they all had different needs. They ranged from Lucas, Vick's five-time fighting champion who was friendly, goofy, and in your face to Meryl, who was terrified of her own shadow. We had to earn her confidence, and we had to work to get her to trust humans. These dogs, which other people had deemed irreparably broken, recovered to a remarkable extent.

There is a stigma about fighting dogs that they will attack anything. The fact is, they have been bred, conditioned, and trained to kill other dogs, not people. People who engage in dog fighting are their caretakers—and they are certainly not good caretakers—but their dogs don't bite the hand that feeds them. Breeders of fighting dogs look for instinctive traits that make a good fighting dog, and they work to perpetuate them. Our job was not to deprogram them; it was to manage them in transition, to enrich their lives and set them up for success. They went from a life of abuse—ripping the flesh off of other dogs, breaking the bones of other dogs, and living on chains—to suddenly living in a place that met their basic needs, with natural light, running water, fresh drinking water, bedding, and likely the first veterinary care of their lives. That's when we started to see these dogs flourish. The dogs were smart enough to figure out that they were in a good place, and they began to turn into companion animals—with restrictions, of course. These were not dogs you could take to a dog park.

Before they came to WARL, a court had deemed the eleven Vick dogs unadoptable and likely, in a legalistic term, irreparable.

They left our shelter different dogs. But that is not to say a fighting dog will be free of issues. They require a different type of management. Most dogs that show aggression do so against something specific: a certain size of dog or being approached by a dog in a certain way. Dogfighting dogs are bred, conditioned, and trained to kill other dogs. I do not believe it is appropriate to call them vicious or even aggressive, for these words imply malicious intent, and humans are the only species of animal capable of that.

Fighting dogs can be adopted, but they must go to an adopter who has the capacity, experience, and resources to manage the situation. This is likely not a dog who is going to doggie day care. This is a dog who may live the rest of his life without contact with other dogs. Assessing, training, reconditioning, and working with abused animals is a long process, not a determination that can be made by assessments while the animals are still in transition. An assessment is a snapshot in time. For that reason, you will never see an animal labeled "aggressive" in one of my emergency shelters, even if that dog is showing signs of aggression. We don't want to label him because labels stick, and dogs in our shelters are very much in transition.

Fighting dogs—from organized dogfighting operations—are a rarity in shelters. Dogs don't break from the chains of a secretive, underground activity. More often, shelters will see street fighting dogs. They are accessories of bad guys, and they may have been abused enough to create a fighting temperament. The bad guys will meet in a schoolyard or a park at two in the morning and pit their dogs against each other.

One reason we didn't want the public to know we had the Vick dogs, even though we didn't handle their adoptions, was because we were concerned that a Vick dog would give credibility to someone who added one to his street-fighting stable.

Several years after his arrest, Michael Vick told NBC News that he would like to get a dog. When I saw that story, I returned to the way of thinking that I learned when I had Capone; I processed Vick's statement through the filter of the Vick dogs. Shortly thereafter, I wrote a blog post that summarized my feelings. Because it so captured—and still captures—my feelings and emotions, I am including some of its text here:

> Michael Vick says that his daughter would like a dog. In a recent NBC interview he said, "I miss having a dog right now. My daughters miss having one. And that's the hardest thing, telling them that we can't have one because of my actions."
>
> I personally cared for eleven of Vick's previous dogs—the eleven who were deemed most behaviorally injured. I was then the executive director of the Washington Animal Rescue League. Weeks after Vick was arrested, the court-appointed guardian of the dogs contacted me. She had heard about our progressive facility and was asking my team to begin the rehabilitation process. I agreed, and we at WARL committed ourselves to the special needs of these most vulnerable dogs.
>
> Dog fighting is a horrific illegal blood sport, but our eleven charges were victims of more than dog fights. The prosecutor's record reveals that they lived tortured lives in a gruesome place. They endured agonizing training regimens and fights to survive. Those designated as bait dogs had all forty-two teeth pulled while tied to a rape stand. The rape stand was also used to bind females so they could be forcibly bred. The need to replace dogs who died in fights or who were murdered by Vick and his gang was constant.
>
> Vick himself pled guilty to drowning, electrocuting, hanging, shooting, and beating dogs to death. Evidence reveals that some of the hanging victims died slowly—their feet barely skimming the ground. Some of the drowning victims were shocked, too. Many were savagely beaten. Michael Vick was found to be directly responsible for fighting them, for breaking their bones and spirits.
>
> My attention was focused on rehabilitating our eleven injured souls. WARL is one of the most open and progressive animal shelters in the country. We temporarily restructured several

living areas to help the victims feel safe, and in fact to ensure their anonymity during the judicial process. WARL received no money for caring for these dogs; we did it because it was the right thing to do.

When we assessed them to identify their individual needs we found dogs who were broken both physically and emotionally. Their bones were shattered, ears were cut off, lips were ripped and massive scabs covered their bodies. They bore homemade sutures. Their collars were so tight they had to be cut off. The bath water that washed over their scarred bodies ran black.

When I looked at the Vick dogs, they cowered and I could see the terror in their eyes—hoping and yet afraid to trust. One dog refused to eat for weeks, trembling whenever a caretaker approached her. Joy was unknown to her, and she was wary of our kindness.

We began the painstaking rehabilitation process, immersing each dog with an individualized enrichment plan. Soon "the Vick Dogs" became our dogs: Georgia, Lucas, Denzel, Willie, Meryl, Ellen, Layla, Charlie, Sweet Pea, Sweet Jasmine, and Tug.

During the next several months, my staff and I came to know these dogs intimately. The cruelty that they endured is unimaginable; the healing power of genuine compassion—miraculous. I will always be in awe of their courage to risk trusting humans once again.

Michael Vick says that his daughter would like a dog. He said, "I would love to get another dog in the future. I think it would be a big step for me in the rehabilitation process. I think just to have a pet in my household and to show people that I genuinely care, and my love and my passion for animals."

I believe in second chances. I've learned about genuine forgiveness and rehabilitation from the best. "The Eleven" were given a second chance and I saw them heal.

Michael Vick? His words, though well-coached, still say it's all about him. I'm still waiting to hear him say how sorry he is for torturing and killing dogs. I'm waiting for him to take personal responsibility for his crimes. I'm waiting for him to admit that childhood culture isn't the cause of his ignorance. I'm waiting for him to say his deeds were truly unforgivable.

I am not qualified to determine whether a criminal is reha-
bilitated, nor am I qualified to talk about Vick as an individual.
In my career in animal protection, I have come across thousands
of animal abusers, and I still do not understand how their minds
work, how they can possibly commit such horrific acts. I strongly
believe that convicted animal abusers forfeit the privilege of caring for animals ever again. Heavy lifetime restrictions are placed
upon violent offenders toward humans; surely they should also
be placed upon those who are violent toward animals.

My life's mission is to elevate the status of animals and to be
with them on the journey to their rightful place in our world. I
believe in their right to live a life free from the suffering caused
by human hands.

Some people are supporting Michael Vick's desire for a dog.

Not me.

We took on the Vick dogs with the expectation that we would
set them up for success, a goal I never doubted we would reach—
and we did.

During the time I had the Vick dogs in my care, I got a visit at
WARL from Wayne Pacelle, the president and chief executive officer
of the Humane Society of the United States. We had known each
other for years at a distance and showed respect for each other's
work, but had never been close. "You've done great things here,"
Wayne told me. "Your work has been stellar. It's time we shined a
spotlight on your work and give you a national platform."

With that, he asked me to come to HSUS as the senior director of its animal rescue team. I would build a strike team and rescue animals internationally. I would be in charge of the response to
natural disasters as well as the response to human-made disasters,
such as puppy mills. I would be given the authority, on an international level, to oversee every aspect of HSUS's animal cruelty cases
and natural disaster responses.

I knew that my challenges were over at WARL, and it was time
to move on. I think Wayne knew that, too. I told him I needed a little
time to consider the offer, but in my mind, I accepted immediately.

Just as I didn't choose to make the renovated WARL a career path, I didn't go into the Humane Society of the United States thinking it was my goal of all goals. Nor did I want to go there to rest on someone else's laurels. I went there bound and determined to create change, to make a rescue team second to none.

HSUS was like nothing I had ever done before. I had never worked for an organization as large as this one, with five hundred staff members who were far removed from what I was doing. I had never, for that matter, worked in an office building. A cubicle farm might as well have been a distant planet. It was a culture shock. I had a hard time operating within bureaucracy.

When I left WARL, I told its board I was going to put an end to puppy mills. Straight out of the gate, I began dismantling all that I could. My department, which was used to deploying two or three times a year on natural disasters, now found itself deploying fifty times a year.

I had strong resources in my department—equipment and a team I was able to develop, not to mention the fact that I didn't have to worry about raising funds for cases. I also had the resources of the HSUS, which included state directors across the country: people who were in charge of building relationships with the authorities we assisted on cases. For the most part, we didn't conduct investigations or build cases. Law enforcement called us in to provide support for rescue, care, and placement.

My first deployment for HSUS, just weeks after I started, came in the aftermath of a tornado in Macon County, Tennessee, northeast of Nashville.

After that I led what is still considered to be the largest puppy mill raid in American history, in August 2008, in Parkersburg, West Virginia. Over three days, we extracted 973 animals, which turned into more than 1,000, as litters were delivered in the emergency shelter—a warehouse just down the street from the local humane society. The dogs were small, Dachshunds mostly, but there were also Yorkies, King Charles Cavalier Spaniels, and Poodles. Most of the dogs were in rabbit hutches strewn outside. There were four buildings that all resembled the buildings we see so often: outdoor hutches connected to whelping boxes.

The puppy mill owner surrendered 100 percent of the dogs on the first day, despite her initial efforts to hang onto some.

At one point, the puppy mill owner sent her husband out to cut down a tree that she hoped would fall on us. We had a pretty good idea what was happening when the leaves began to shake and we heard a chainsaw, and asked a deputy to investigate. Moments later, the husband walked in our direction, with the still-running saw in his hands. He claimed it was a joke, but it was a joke that earned him a pair of handcuffs.

It's difficult to say which rescues I am the proudest of having led. So much goes into any one of them. There are personal components and problems to overcome. I measure my success based on the quantity of lives saved and the quality with which that action was performed. I seek to save as many lives as possible and inspire change in the process. It's that simple. But I also remember the cases where we came in the nick of time.

We were called in for a horse case in Cannon County, Tennessee. I was particularly interested in this mission because I previously knew very little about horses. It was a case about a dealer, a man who bought and sold horses for slaughter, possibly for meat, to be sold in other countries. Because of the fate he had in mind, he didn't worry about feeding them. If a horse was too sick for his commercial uses, the man had his employees dig a hole with a backhoe and bury the horse alive. When we arrived on his property with law enforcement officials, hoping to have a look around, the owner told us to go fuck ourselves, which meant that law enforcement had to spend several hours obtaining a search warrant. When we finally entered the property, steps behind the officials carrying the warrant, he told us again to go fuck ourselves. Soon he was under arrest, and we got to work rescuing animals—Tennessee Walking Horses, Spotted Saddle Horses, and quarter horses. To assess their conditions, we used a widely respected scale, the Henneke Body Condition Scoring System.

Devised by the late Don Henneke, PhD, in 1983 when he was a graduate student at Texas A&M University, the system is based around six areas of the horse most responsive to change in body fat: the neck, withers, shoulder, ribs, loin, and tailhead. It replaced value judgments, such as "skinny" or "fat," with a scale of one through nine. A one denotes an emaciated horse with little or no body fat. A nine is obese. A body score between four and seven is considered acceptable; a five is ideal.

All of the horses in our case were ones or twos. Their ribs stuck out like washboards. Many could stand but not walk. Mothers could not produce enough milk to feed their foals. They were living skeletons. In addition to the extreme emaciation, we found horses suffering from a variety of medical ailments including overgrown, infected hooves and parasite infestation. We found dead horses, but we saved all of the living.

The case started around Thanksgiving and continued for the better part of two months, until the horses were all healthy enough to be transported to placement partners. We shouldn't have been able to save eighty-four starving horses, but somehow we did. On a daily basis, a few of them, too sick to carry their own weight, would drop to the ground. A horse in such terrible condition will most often die within thirty minutes of being on the ground. And a horse, even a skeletal one, is no easy animal to get to his feet. Some of the horse people working with us knew what to do: slide two objects under the downed horse—perhaps two posts—and then four people on each side would lift the horse up. The local fire department got wind of our work and stationed people at the shelter to be part of the team. They donated old fire hoses, cut the caps of off them, and created our primary horse-lifting tools. Not a day went by without up to a dozen horses falling. There was a particular sound we would hear when a horse hit the ground. No matter where we were in the emergency shelter, we would hear that "thunk" and run. Knowing the urgency made the accomplishment of getting a horse back on her feet even sweeter.

I recently learned about one of the Cannon County horses who went to a rescue group, which adopted out the horse. The horse wound up being rescued a second time, in another cruelty case. I am happy that the horse is alive and well, but I had a difficult time knowing that one of the horses whose suffering I made a promise to end wound up suffering again. That was a really hard story to swallow. The fact that my system failed that horse disturbs me, but it was another learning experience that made us better.

Making sure everything went right was one of our responsibilities. And that meant seeking out and hiring the best employees. Whenever possible, part of my interview process at HSUS was to take a job candidate on a rescue. Most of them failed that test. That test also brought me Karla Goodson on a sweltering August day in Kaufman County, Texas.

Karla had followed my career path for quite some time. She had been a volunteer for Washington Animal Rescue League while still in college. She attended a conference of Taking Action for Animals, where I spoke. She introduced herself and told me she was going to work for me.

I knew I was going to hire her before her working interview on the Texas rescue was even completed. She excelled.

We removed nearly six hundred dogs from some of the most deplorable of conditions. On a scale of one to ten, this was a ten.

The dogs were mostly small breeds, including Chihuahuas, toy Poodles, Beagles, and Yorkshire Terriers. We found dogs suffering from the full menu of puppy mill maladies: severely matted fur, skin infections, eye infections, parasites, fleas, and infected wounds. But that was only the beginning. We encountered dead and dying animals, and some still-living animals who were being eaten by maggots.

That day Karla showed me all I needed to know about her potential as an animal rescuer. She was tough. She stood up to one of our worst situations. But she also showed, in an account she wrote about the day, what was in her heart:

> This dog, who was so matted and covered in feces it was hard to identify her breed, was existing (for you certainly could not call it living) in the worst of the buildings at the puppy mill. The oppressive heat inside pressed into your body and the ammonia immediately burned your nose and eyes. The barking of hundreds of dogs crowded into wire cages was non-stop. No senses were safe from the misery that was everywhere, and for these dogs that hell had been inescapable.
>
> We had already pulled many dogs to safety and were in the "rescue zone." I was ready for Scotlund to hand me another dog but we had to pause when we came to one particular old girl who was among three hundred-some dogs suffering in that single building. I got to the doorway and saw him pull a dog, whom I thought was dead, out from under a stack of cages, hold her for a moment and say, "I just don't know what to say about this." She showed painfully obvious signs of the toll puppy mills take on breeding mothers—her old, emaciated, filthy body suffering the effects of years of neglect and endless breeding.
>
> Scotlund asked me if I was ready for her and as he placed this fragile dog gently into my arms I said, "Come on, babe." That was probably the first affectionate name she was ever called, the first time she was ever handled lovingly and the first time she was considered as an individual. The dog who came to be known as Babe died just minutes later in our arms. After years of producing litter after litter she lay hidden and forgotten, left to die, until we came for her. She had held on long enough to experience respect and compassion. Babe will not only always represent for me the horrors of a puppy mill but also the resilience of dogs and the patient, forgiving love of mothers.

A custody hearing for the animals from the Karla-initiation case took place the week after our rescue. A proceeding of this sort usually takes an hour. This one took two days. A courtroom that would normally have been virtually empty was full of my volunteers, who were invested in the results. The puppy mill operator represented herself. She was unkempt and disheveled. The distinctive smell of a puppy mill was oozing out of her pores, and she tried to discredit our collective work. I had testified that we found rough-hewn wire cages stacked one on top of the other, leaving a clear path for one dog's excrement to drop onto the dog below. On the second day of the hearing, the puppy mill operator produced a piece of linoleum she had slid between two cages as a makeshift floor. This, she told the judge, was what she used between all of her cages, seemingly believing she could prove, with one purported exception to my testimony, that the case against her was baseless. As soon as she produced that piece of linoleum, the entire courtroom recoiled from the odor. "What is that smell?" asked the judge. "Do you realize you're not helping yourself here?"

The puppy mill operator lost custody of the dogs. She was charged, convicted, and put on probation.

Not quite two years later, on Animal Rescue Corps's second case, we caught wind that this puppy mill was back in operation. We shut her down again, and this time we rescued forty-nine dogs. The operator was in jail for Mother's Day.

In Operation Autumn Angels, ARC removed more than sixty dogs from severely neglectful conditions at a breeding operation in Mississippi. All of the dogs from the October 2015 mission were turned over to ARC.

Amiee Stubbs

I do not view one animal's life as more important than another's. Animal Rescue Corps has been called on to assist numerous species.

Amiee Stubbs

Humane education is an integral part of ARC's mission. Through our two-day Basic Animal Rescue Course, we teach people how to respond to animal cruelty in their communities, and we expand the cadre of volunteers who join us on large-scale cases.

Amiee Stubbs

Puppy mills come in all shapes and sizes, but this scene is sadly typical of a great many: row after row of solitary confinement.

Rich Folkers carries one of 132 dogs ARC rescued during
operation Liberty Dogs on July 3, 2014, in rural Virginia.

Amiee Stubbs

Members of the ARC crew and volunteers from the BISSELL Pet Foundation
get together for a group picture after a day of rescues during
Operation Spring Break in Illinois in April 2015.

Amiee Stubbs

Structure is critical during ARC's rescue operations, for the safety of both animals and people. We begin each mission with a briefing and review of an organizational chart that lays out every job and who reports to whom.

Kim Rezac cuts the chain from one of twelve dogs ARC rescued from a dog-fighting property in Mississippi in April 2014 during Operation Delta Dogs.

Amiee Stubbs

A dog from a dogfighting operation comes close to embrace a gentle human touch for what is likely the first time in his life. The resilience of dogs, even in the most dispiriting of conditions, inspires me to persevere.

Amiee Stubbs

One of the most dispiriting places in a puppy mill is an outbuilding we often find containing breeding mothers and newborn puppies. This building, from Operation Unbridled Spirit in September 2013 in Kentucky, had heavy levels of ammonia and virtually no ventilation.

ARC staff and volunteers pose with law enforcement officers after they raided a dogfighting operation in Mississippi in April 2014. Just hours earlier, the chains and posts in front of them held a dozen fighting dogs.

Music and art remain important parts of my life. In this image I am sitting in front of what is often called The Wall of Cash, a mural in Nashville honoring the late Johnny Cash, a musician I admire and the subject of several of my own paintings.

Carol Guzy

In the aftermath of Hurricane Katrina, a week after the levees broke, a team from the Washington Animal Rescue League joined other animal welfare groups and first responders in the devastated, flooded city. Through long days and nights, in excruciating conditions, our sole focus was on rescuing animals like this dog from the Faubourg Marigny neighborhood.

Carol Guzy

Many of the animals we rescued following Hurricane Katrina in New Orleans were, like this dog, clinging to life, so weakened from dehydration and hunger that they could barely stand.

My art is inspired by the suffering and salvation I witness during my animal rescue work. Lucas, in this painting, is one of the eleven dogs seized during the Michael Vick dogfighting case that we cared for and worked to rehabilitate at the Washington Animal Rescue League during Vick's trial.

Justin Leonard

ARC rescued eighteen chickens, including roosters, hens, and chicks, and two cats from a closed-down trailer park in a suburb of Baltimore, in October 2015. The animals had been fending for themselves for weeks after residents moved out and abandoned them.

CHAPTER NINE

THE JOURNEY CONTINUES

Over time, I came to believe that I might be more effective creating my own organization with a focused agenda. By concentrating on a limited number of priorities, an organization can put 100 percent effort toward every issue, rather than being spread thin over a spectrum of agendas.

When I left HSUS, I held a conference call with my team to give them the news. By then, we had built a group with some solid members, most of whom were surprised at my departure. But it was Karla who came to me and asked, "Where are we going next?" There was no hesitation. She was all in, wherever the road led.

During a social get-together at an Irish pub, I revealed to a small group of confidantes that I planned to start Animal Rescue Corps. "We're starting our own organization?" Karla asked. "Hell, yeah."

While I was developing plans for what is now Animal Rescue Corps, I took a temporary position in June 2010 as the interim president of a California-based group called In Defense of Animals, or IDA. The organization was founded in 1983 by Dr. Eliot Katz, who at the time of my appointment was stepping back from day-to-day leadership but retaining the board chairmanship. In assessing the organization, I sat down with each person in its employ, to get his perspective. One of those meetings began with the employee saying, "May I be candid?" He then continued to explain in eloquent, professional detail how he would make the organization stronger and more vital. He told me he thought he was more capable than others recognized, and he wanted to be part of making the organization better. I immediately promoted him and made him my right hand at IDA. Later, Tim Woodward (along with his husband, Michael) completed the core of the leadership of the newfound ARC.

As I moved past the temporary position at IDA, the pieces of my new organization came together quickly. But nearly a year passed before any of us took a salary. It wasn't supposed to be that way.

We had established an initial budget of $300,000 to launch ARC. We had a meeting of a small board of directors on November 7, 2010, and invited two potential donors as advisers. One of them committed to the full amount we needed. He called me a couple of days later and said, "Listen, you're not starting this organization without me. I'm a significant player, and I want equal billing with you as co-founder. I want it fifty-fifty."

I didn't respond. I told Tim about the proposition, and he replied with a sentence I will never forget: "The co-founder position is not for sale."

I went back to the donor and declined his offer. I think he knew that would be my response, but he told me, "Good luck getting the money on your own," and hung up.

I had no choice but to go to Tim and tell him that I could not fulfill my financial commitment to our fledgling organization. We'll figure it out, he said, and we started the organization anyway.

We raised funds, which went toward our first rescue, a puppy mill in Warren County, Tennessee. I assembled the rest of the team out of volunteers I had gotten to know during my career in protecting animals.

It was Tim's first on-scene rescue. He had worked for animal causes, but had never been in the field. I didn't see a lot of emotion from him that day, but I could see he had no regrets for the sacrifices he was making for the organization. The fact that he and Karla put their trust in me and in a nearly penniless organization is something for which I will be forever grateful. We didn't even get hotels rooms for the initial stages of that rescue; we slept on volunteers' floors.

A great deal has happened since those early days of ARC, and in what seems like the blink of an eye, we are now more than five years old. We had no name or identity in our infancy as an organization-to-be. The "animal rescue" in our name was easy. We called ourselves a "corps" because the word comes from the Latin "corpus," or body, as in an organized body of people. "Corps" has been used in the names of many organizations, including the Peace Corps, the Marine Corps, and Mercy Corps. Animal Rescue Corps would become a corps of compassion.

ARC also was the perfect acronym for the organization we worked to build, and the embodiment of a quote from the Reverend Dr. Martin Luther King, Jr.: "The arc of the moral universe is long, but it bends towards justice."

ARC's logo features a pair of abstract wings. The words "animal rescue" are outlined in a yellow box, the word "corps" outlined in a yellow triangle. The logo was a collaborative effort by our team, not the result of a marketing firm's work. We chose the Helvetica font because of its simple, straightforward ubiquity—a font familiar to most everyone. The yellow triangle around "corps" represents the three points of the words rescue, recover, and re-home. We opted to use wings rather than a representation of an animal to symbolically represent the lifting up of all animals—and to be our ARC angel wings. We call our monthly donors ARC Angels.

Two months after ARC launched, in March 2011, we were on the scene of that puppy mill in Warren County, Tennessee. The old, familiar smell was all too apparent when we arrived. Walking onto the property, we passed a series of signs. One read, "Warning: Do not approach animals without owners' consent! Any accident that occurs is not the responsibility of the owner." Another was a bit more terse: "Don't even think about coming in here." Up the hundred-foot driveway was a fifty-year-old puppy mill.

Structures were scattered haphazardly throughout the property, with no thoughtful design. Outbuildings were carved into the thick of the woods, hanging over a stream, and even mounted to the side of the house. Once the puppy mill operator ran out of structures, she began using her basement. This is where the majority of the nursing mothers and puppies were kept.

We began our work after three in the afternoon, as the process of getting a warrant had been time-consuming. Daylight would be fleeting, so we focused first on the outside.

Like most any puppy mill we raid, we weren't sure of the number of dogs we were about to find. As our team removed sheets of plastic that covered rusted, filthy rabbit hutches full of dogs, we quickly estimated that more than a hundred dogs were languishing in wire mesh cages encrusted with feces and urine. We had to cut some of them out; their fur had grown into and virtually melded with the cage and the accumulated feces. The total came to one hundred twenty one living dogs and seven that were deceased. One young pup had actually been using two of his dead cage mates as a blanket.

It is important to note that while this operation happened in ARC's infancy, we operated as if we had been together for years. We were organized and efficient and, thanks to many volunteers, moved like the compassionate army we are.

Before we could enter the house, officials called in a hazardous materials team to clear the air. The ammonia stench was overpowering. Dogs' eyes were filmed over, burned from living in the toxic air for years on end.

The cruelty of this place and its half-century history of starvation, neglect, untreated wounds, and death couldn't have been more obvious. Yet none of those things got this property condemned. Rather, it was the fact that one of the buildings on the property was above a running creek that became contaminated by feces dropping from the cages. That's what got us to this place, legally, and it demonstrates one of the ways ARC is most effective: We use every avenue of the law to save lives.

The District Attorney of Warren County was quick to respond. The office doesn't tolerate cruelty to animals, and it didn't hesitate to mobilize resources. The dedication to justice of law enforcement and prosecutors allow us to do what we do.

We finished our work at two in the morning, adding five exotic birds to our rescued total.

Once we had them out of the mill, the animals went straight to ARC's emergency shelter, which this time we set up on the Tennessee State Fairgrounds. Medical stations addressed critical injuries and general health needs; groomers removed inches of feces-matted and flea-infested fur; and volunteers spent time socializing each dog, offering affection for at least fifteen minutes, two to three times each day.

All of the dogs went to placement partners, on the road to finding forever homes.

For ARC, it was proof of the principle that compassion combined with professionalism and structured operation is the best way to get the job done and create a lasting solution. We also could not function without the commitment of volunteers. They inspire me, and they also put in long days of difficult work in challenging conditions. If you want to understand just what that cadre of volunteers means, you need look no further than Operation Mending Hearts.

On a Friday in February, at approximately five o'clock in the afternoon, ARC received a call from officials in Hamblen County, Tennessee, asking for help with an urgent situation. The local humane society had discovered more than seventy animals living in deplorable conditions, and they needed assistance with the operation.

Mobilizing for action on a Friday evening is a challenge, to be sure. This one was a higher hurdle, for this particularly Friday in February was Valentine's Day. I knew that most people—my staff and my volunteers—would be heading out for an evening with a loved one. But it was equally clear that these animals could not wait. I sent out an email request, and within twenty minutes, I had ARC's Tennessee volunteer response team and other members of ARC's leadership on a conference call. We discussed the situation, devised a plan, and charged each person with tasks to make a quick response possible. No one hesitated. No one complained. Every one of our volunteers spent the rest of Valentine's Day deploying other team members, securing transport vehicles, preparing an emergency shelter, and getting equipment and supplies ready. Because of their dedication, we were assembled in Tennessee a mere twenty-two hours after receiving the phone call from law enforcement.

On the property, we found dozens of animals without access to food and water, surrounded by piles of garbage, feces, and filth. Dogs, including several nursing mothers, were trapped in small, soiled cages stacked high on top of each other. We discovered dogs with extreme dehydration and signs of injuries, illnesses, and internal and external parasites. Yet the volunteers at my side did not flinch; they did not pause to catch their breath. Faced with a heartbreaking and horrific scene, the team focused solely on ending the suffering of the animals and our mission to deliver them to safety.

Volunteers assembled housing and prepared intake forms. Other team members carried animals out of their hideous conditions. Hours passed, temperatures dropped, and volunteers worked tirelessly. Just after midnight, I removed the final dog, a beautiful black lab mix, from a dark, damp cellar. As snow began to fall, we paused for a moment to celebrate the rescue of seventy-three dogs and two cats. It was a short pause, because our work was far from over. We drove three and a half hours to Lebanon, Tennessee, to our emergency shelter, where another team of ARC volunteers had spent the day and night setting up. Though exhausted, our volunteers worked into the early hours of the morning, fueled by the relief of knowing that these frightened, tired animals would finally be able to rest. Operation Mending Hearts was a success.

I started ARC with the intention of creating an organization that was volunteer-driven. Never could I have imagined the amazing response we would receive. We now have thousands of volunteers across North America, and they are the most selfless and compassionate group of individuals I have ever had the great honor to work with. Knowing that I have volunteers so driven and committed to seeking justice for the forgotten, people who would drop any and every plan at the last minute to serve without rest or reward, reminds me that while I see the worst humanity has to offer on these operations, I also see the very best.

Many of the volunteers went home that night to sleep for only a few hours before returning to care for the needs of the animals and help veterinary teams provide medical care for each one. None of these volunteers was working for payment or special recognition. Many of them have families and full-time jobs. They all have additional responsibilities and a number of other ways they could have spent their weekend—but their compassion drives them to serve. They believe so strongly in ending suffering that their own fatigue fades when they see an animal finally close his eyes to rest. They set their personal interests aside when they witness the heartache of an animal that has been denied the life he was meant to live. And the most beautiful part is this: As a volunteer's selfless compassion heals these precious charges, she is richly rewarded by witnessing the animal's resilience—and his power to love again.

If we think about our actions that directly or indirectly affect others, human or non-human, it is clear that all negative actions are unwelcome. Often these negative behaviors are encouraged or sanctioned by society, tradition, or corporate marketing, making it easier for us as individuals to choose not to think about our actions or about their repercussions. There is always someone ready to do the dirty work for profit, hiding much of the ugliness and making it convenient to ignore. Most consumers don't think about the enslaved children who make cheap clothes or the other unethical measures some businesses take to offer us a product or service at "the lowest possible cost."

Great efforts are made to hide from view the suffering of people and animals exploited by unscrupulous industries because that knowledge and awareness would force each of us to accept responsibility for playing a role in that suffering. If we choose to remain ignorant, our lives may be easier or more convenient in the short term, but our ignorance will always be at another living being's expense, a being who was also born to live in this world and who is as deserving of an opportunity to live a valued life as we are.

I believe we all play a role and share a responsibility to create a society that values all life. I am told daily that I speak for the voiceless. I don't. I take action against injustice. I do it directly through my work at ARC and, as importantly, through the daily decisions I make. I believe that the endless, seemingly unimportant decisions we all make every day can make the greatest difference in creating the society we wish to see, particularly if those decisions are informed and made with thoughtfulness and respect for all.

Some of the practices I have adopted include reading the ingredients of everything and choosing not to consume animal products; buying sustainable and cruelty-free products; researching the origin of products, when possible; and trying to always make compassionate and respectful choices. Giving more thought to the decisions I make is to me the basis of being about change. There isn't such a thing as perfection, but there can be a sense of enjoyment in always learning more and allowing that knowledge to guide us in making ever better and better decisions.

Better choices can, at times, mean sacrificing convenience. We may have to spend a little more money, look a little harder, or wait a little longer to find a compassionate option for a product, but the value of being informed and knowing that our decisions correspond with our values is not something that can be measured in dollars. We are what we consume, and our societal consumption today is not sustainable—and often borne from the suffering of others. As compassionate individuals our actions are filled with contradictions, but when we put our contradictions on trial, meaning becomes clearer, making change possible. We must think before we act; we must ignite change by being the change.

There are people in the animal protection world, past and present, whom I consider heroes. They have given of themselves to improve the lot of animals everywhere. One of the people I hold out as a true visionary and hero in all things is Dr. King. His wisdom was both before its time and long past due in a world that desperately needed his message of justice and compassion for all, as well as his example of persistence and hope.

I believe no limit should exist on who deserves consideration and protection; half a century after Dr. King shared his dream with us, the need is still extensive. Men, women, and children of every race, creed, nationality, and sexuality around the world are still victims of prejudice and oppression. Non-human animals also suffer—too often valued for their profitability and not for the intrinsic beauty they bring to the world. Though there has been incredible progress for many, we still have a long way to go until suffering has ended and all are "free at last."

The struggle for justice and equality is not easy, but it is within our power to make change. Though we can't see what the future holds, we are driven to end suffering as we steadfastly follow our collective moral compass. The belief that change is possible is essential to my motivation to continue defending animals. Dr. King's determined insight is ARC's guiding light in our mission to end animal suffering through direct and compassionate action.

Dr. King's strong and hopeful words of justice and compassion transcend time and, though his focus was civil rights, also transcend species. He once said, "One day the absurdity of the almost universal human belief in the slavery of other animals will be palpable. We shall then have discovered our souls and become worthier of sharing this planet with them."

Dr. King believed in nonviolence and connectedness. In April 1963, when he was jailed in Birmingham, Alabama, for his part in planning peaceful protests, he wrote, "Injustice anywhere is a threat to justice everywhere." I also believe the suffering of one is the concern of all, and that we must broaden our empathies to include all who are capable of suffering. Everyone working against injustice must not only support others within our own movements, but also champion the causes of other compassionate crusades. Whether we are fighting for women's rights, marriage equality, LGBT rights, animal protection, or one of the many other social causes worth defending, we share the basic belief that justice should be blind and the common goal that inequity and suffering be defeated. We are all making progress in our movements; together we can make large and lasting change for all. To this end, ARC sees the immense value in bringing people together. We work with local and national authorities, other animal protection organizations, and members of the communities where we rescue animals because collaboration is critical to success.

I find strength and motivation in the dynamic example of Dr. King, and I hope to honor his legacy by inspiring others to join me in advancing positive change on our way to a just world. As Dr. King said, "A great nation is a compassionate nation," and I will not stop fighting until justice and compassion has been achieved for all.

When you spend your life confronting the horrible things people are capable of doing to animals, it isn't always easy to follow the lessons Dr. King taught us. Compassion is a gift we share. It is my source of inspiration and strength. But living our beliefs asks much of us.

While I was an animal control officer, I received a call on a beautiful spring day to respond to a dog beating in progress in a Capitol Hill neighborhood. I raced through the city and arrived, within minutes, at the address. I learned, from conversations on the radio, that police already had a suspect in custody a few blocks away. My job was to tend to the injured dog and his family. I looked up and saw a man crying in the front yard, hugging close the lifeless twelve-pound body of a Lhasa Apso. He was inconsolable. With some patience and persistence, I learned the story of what had transpired.

Penny, the Lhasa Apso, was sunning herself in her fenced-in front yard when a man and his three-year-old daughter entered the yard of the house next door. The man left his daughter in the front yard while he went inside to visit a female companion. The daughter walked over to the fence to say hello to Penny and stuck her hand through to pet the dog. Penny nipped at the little girl, who then began to cry. The girl's father emerged from the house, saw his crying daughter and saw Penny at the fence. He began screaming at the dog. Penny's guardian heard the commotion and called out the window that he was on his way outside. By the time he arrived in his front yard, the little girl's father had beaten Penny to death with a board from his fence. The suspect fled the scene, leaving his daughter behind.

This case took two years to prosecute, but the authorities, Penny's guardian, and I were all dedicated to justice. The trial lasted for two days. Penny's guardian was physically shaken after giving his testimony; the loss of his beloved companion still haunted him—and me. We all sat with clenched hands as the judge prepared to read her verdict. The man who beat Penny to death was sentenced to three years in prison, the maximum penalty for his crime.

Penny, her guardian, the police, and the court system reaffirmed my belief in the power of justice through collaboration. That sense of honor and humility toward those I protect has remained a guiding principle of my life's work. And as much as I am repulsed by the actions of abusers, my duty in following the example of Dr. King is to work for change without bearing hate against the abuser.

CHAPTER TEN

PIT BULLS AND CHICKENS

Abuse is all too common in our world, transcending people and animals. I can think of no animal species that does not suffer at the hands of people. In my career, I have rescued multiple species, including dogs, cats, exotic and wild birds, horses, non-human primates, rabbits, rodents, farmed animals, and multiple other exotic, wild, and domestic animals. I have led rescue operations of road-side zoos, dog- and cock-fighting cases, pet stores, hoarding cases, puppy mills, research labs, fur farms, backyard farms, and more. Of all the suffering I have witnessed, of numerous species, the most abused animal, in my view, is the chicken and the most abused companion animal is the pit bull.

Let's start with pit bulls. Of all the highly charged, hot-button topics that concern me, one that rises to the top is breed-specific legislation.

Breed-specific legislation, or BSL, as these laws are collectively known, would ban certain dog breeds that are assumed to be dangerous to society. The dog most often subject to bans today is known as the pit bull. I phrase it that way because, technically, "pit bull" is not a breed; it is a term categorizing a strong and athletic class of terriers that most popularly includes the American Staffordshire Terrier and the American Pit Bull Terrier.

These breeds are subjected to bans because there is widespread prejudice based on the common misunderstanding of their temperament. Indeed, pit bulls are used for fighting and other nefarious activities because of their determined and courageous nature. Yet that very same tenacity can make pit bulls outstanding members of family, community, police, and military groups. The typically resourceful pit bull cheerfully assumes the duties that life requires of him. Human guardians are responsible for positively directing the focus of the dog's spirit and not taking advantage of it for unethical purposes. It is the negative manipulation of the pit bull nature that has given birth to the unfair reputation of the breeds.

Back in my animal control days, I participated in a heart-wrenching episode that highlights pit bull prejudice, and also reveals the purity of a child's wisdom. The saga began at dusk when a man heard a noise coming from the far side of his car, which was parked in the street. He glimpsed movement and demanded that the person come forward, threatening to send his pit bull to attack if that individual failed to surrender. The hidden figure stayed frozen in place; the man incited his dog to leave his property and attack. The man then heard screams and followed his dog, only to discover him mauling a ten-year-old girl. He called off the dog, but the little girl was bleeding profusely and critically injured.

I was called to the scene to take control of the dog while the girl was rushed away in an ambulance and the man arrested. The dog, who was impounded and restricted from human contact for more than a year, was named Face. I came to know Face over a significant amount of time prior to the hearing that would decide his fate. Face was sweet, but his eagerness to please had been taken advantage of and manipulated. He had been obeying his guardian's urgent command to protect him by attacking the perceived danger. The little girl who had been injured, as well as the dog, who would be killed for doing what the person he trusted most had asked of him, saddened me greatly. Both the dog and the child were victims of a person who abused his power.

I visited the girl in the hospital, hoping to ease her emotional pain. I told her that the courts were going to make a decision about whether Face would be deemed a "dangerous dog" and lose his life. This child, who required plastic surgery, told me to ask the court not to punish Face. She said, "It isn't the dog's fault. It's the man's fault for teaching his dog bad things and using him that way."

She got it exactly right. It is the nature of the pit bull to persevere and endure. This drive is not related to innate aggression, but is instead related to learned behaviors born of their loyalty and the drive to successfully complete assigned tasks, despite adversity.

Historically, pit bull breeds have enjoyed a positive public image. They were trusted as beloved family companions. They worked beside farmers at home and soldiers abroad. Their sentimental place in society inspired the character Petey in The Little Rascals, Tige in the Buster Brown comic strip, and more. Helen Keller and Theodore Roosevelt enjoyed the company of a pit bull companion, and a pit bull named Sergeant Stubby still bears the honor as the most decorated service dog in American military history.

Unfortunately, pit bulls have also historically been abused. The term "pit bull" comes from their ancestral use in pits for bull-baiting or fights with other dogs in pits. The media began to build negative pit bull perceptions with articles like an extensive July 1987 *Sports Illustrated* story featuring a cover photograph of a snarling pit bull, with the headline, "Beware of This Dog."

I recall a case in which a Labrador mix dog attacked an elderly gentleman, requiring him to seek emergency treatment. A local paper reported the incident in one article. Soon thereafter, a mixed-breed dog bit a child, sending him to the hospital. Again, the local newspaper printed one article. A few days later, two pit bulls attacked a woman and her dog. The dog was uninjured but the woman was hospitalized. This incident was reported in 230 news articles, as well as on multiple cable news networks.

Extensive misrepresentation of the nature of pit bulls is not merely unfair; it has regrettable consequences. This hype has led to their desirability among individuals seeking personal status or financial gain. The criminal use of pit bulls in professional and amateur dogfights and other illegal activities has ensured the proliferation of the negative stereotype of these dogs. The public is now conditioned to judge the breeds once considered quintessential American dogs as dangerous, and pit bulls are subjected to bans—even if it is a challenge to even define what a pit bull is.

Keeping people and other animals safe from danger must be addressed based on facts rather than emotion. Dog bites can cause serious injuries, even death, and are costly in terms of dollars, community resources, and emotional well-being. But safety isn't achieved by clumsy, blanket restrictions on broad classes of dogs. Reasoning and evidence show that non-specific restrictions affecting enormous numbers of dogs and people are ineffective and inhumane.

A child's wisdom identified the root of the problem: "It isn't the dog's fault. It's the man's fault for teaching his dog bad things and using him that way." The problem is irresponsible guardians. Any solution must address that situation.

Dogs like Face are subjected to manipulative abuse, resulting in extremely distressing outcomes for dogs and humans. Then the dogs are blamed and punished for acting on behalf of their guardian. We should honor the lesson of their suffering by taking proactive stances on how to handle the problems that abused dogs present to society and the problems society presents to them.

Breed-specific legislation is reactive and ineffective, but there are proactive and effective ways to keep humans and dogs safe.

Dogs are born with the instinct to be worthy of their family, to bond with their companion. Determined dogs will serve their guardian's bidding with all of their being. Treated and socialized well, they can become loving family members and readily accepted members of their communities. But if dogs are neglected or manipulated—and encouraged to perform negative behaviors—the consequences for the dogs and humans can be tragic. It is this abuse that is at the root of the dog-human problems that breed-specific legislation attempts.

BSL is not proven to achieve its purported main function: to keep people safe from dog bites. For example, the number of dog bites in Great Britain remained the same despite a ban on three breeds the government classified as pit bulls. The Netherlands enacted a ban on pit bulls in 1993 after three children were killed. The country repealed the law in 2008, saying that it had not solved the dangerous dog problem.

BSL misplaces blame and punishes the innocent. BSL calls for the round-up of all individuals of a certain breed, regardless of whether they have ever bitten anyone. BSL victimizes responsible dog guardians and their companions and imposes societal prejudice against both. Innocent lives are lost and public well-being is hurt by any legislation that wrongly incriminates a majority due to problems with a handful of deviants. BSL doesn't seek to make irresponsible dog guardians liable for their deeds and it doesn't impose penalties on those who commit crimes on animals. Humans who don't socialize or abuse pets too often cause dogs to bite. More than 70 percent of dog bites come from unneutered male dogs, and most fatal dog attacks involve dogs who aren't spayed or neutered. More than 80 percent of dog bites come from dogs who are abused or otherwise recklessly maintained.

BSL is reactive and expensive, blindly applying resources to stick a bandage on a problem, rather than prevent it. Solutions must be proactive and strike at the root of the problem, preventing the potential for dangerous situations to occur, in order to achieve lasting change. BSL costs taxpayers hundreds of thousands of dollars to round up and kill all banned dogs, regardless of their innocence. Prince George's County, Maryland, spends more $250,000 a year to enforce its pit bull ban, even though a 2003 study found that the ban had not improved public safety and that all animal problems were covered by other laws. This money could be spent much more effectively elsewhere. The dogs whose lives are taken and the devastated families who loved them pay a much higher price.

BSL relies on arbitrary breed labels. Most of our nation's 78 million dogs are mixed breeds, thereby defying lineage classification. The term "pit bull" is a generalized description and many dogs who are not pit bulls but share some physical characteristics are unfairly placed in this category.

BSL puts dogs in danger, making banned dogs more desirable to criminals and other irresponsible individuals. Since these individuals can't be seen with the dogs, they keep them in hiding, typically in extreme confinement, sometimes leaving them to starve to death in basements or abandoned buildings. Loving guardians may also hide their banned dogs and forsake daily walks and even veterinary care.

The lovable and loyal pit bull is truly an innocent casualty of discriminatory generalizations that result in illegitimate breed-specific conclusions. The American Temperament Testing Society, an independent research group that has been publishing results since 1977, reports that only one in one thousand pit bulls is "disqualified" due to aggressive tendencies. American Pit Bull Terriers and American Staffordshire Terriers pass temperament tests at a rate of 86 percent and approximately 84 percent, respectively. These rates are similar to or superior to those of Beagles, Golden Retrievers, Jack Russell Terriers, Border Collies, and Standard Poodles.

Yet dog breeds with good reputations find loving homes more easily than dogs labeled as pit bulls. Millions of pit bulls end up in shelters and rescue groups every year. Half or more of the dogs in large city shelters are pit bull types. Small town shelters are also overwhelmed. The results are tragic; the national average death rate of sheltered pit bulls is 93 percent. So for every hundred pit bulls who end up in a shelter, only seven survive. Pit bull breeding is a major contributing factor to this problem and regulations on it must be explored.

BSL cannot address the problems "dangerous dogs" present to society or the problems society presents to dogs. The solutions that will work are not easy and require progressive systems. Regardless, the focus of any action must be on promoting responsible dog guardianship and holding the irresponsible accountable.

One possible solution is pet guardianship regulations—admittedly an ambitious idea, but one worth consideration.

Dogs remain classified as property, and we pay an annual licensing fee for them. However, there is no process to license animal guardians. Driving a car or selling liquor requires people to go through a verification process, in order to be approved by the government. In those cases, citizens need to earn credentials that the government validates, because fellow citizens can be affected by the conduct of each individual. People adopting from an animal shelter should likewise meet certain criteria, because having an animal affects the guardian, the animal, and those around them.

If all animal guardianship required licensing, it would demonstrate—on behalf of the community and on behalf of the animal—that guardianship is a significant responsibility. We could elevate guardianship to an earned privilege. People would have to prove their preparation for the responsibility; they would therefore take the decision to get a companion more seriously because they would be held accountable for that choice.

Guardian licensing legislation wording and implementation would need to be tailored for each community, just as there are differences in animal control and sheltering systems across the country. The entities that would be charged with overseeing a law must be behind it, have an implementation plan in place, and be prepared for its outcomes if it is to be successful. If communities are not supportive or prepared, guardian licensing should not be enacted. If applied responsibly, guardian licensing would keep communities safe and offer a community more than just an alternative to BSL. It would provide a way to directly and proactively address irresponsible guardianship, which humane societies, SPCAs, and shelters are already doing with adoption requirements. It is time to expand these ideas to society as a whole.

While there may be other solutions, it is most definitely time to dismiss discussion of breed-specific legislation. BSL is an abusive idea that doesn't work. It offends common decency and wastes resources and innocent lives.

Even though BSL is flawed, I believe in the judicial system. Laws are written by humans and enforced by humans, and they are subject to human failures. But laws are a critical part of my work, and I believe in structures that are put in place to make our society better. I believe in the concept of creating a structure and abiding by it. Cows, horses, pigs, chickens, minks, and other animals considered agriculture don't have the legal protections that dogs and cats have in the U.S. But using cruelty laws to end cruelty is just one of my techniques. Environmental protection laws, code enforcement, and tax laws, for example, can apply to almost any animal operation.

Getting the issues of animal suffering that we address into as many households as possible creates awareness of industries that directly abuse animals or sponsor cruelty, and leads to change, through laws or simply through personal decisions. If our work leads to local legislation designed to prevent abuse, we will provide our videos and photographs and I am happy to testify. ARC does not lobby or work to change laws, but we will always support those who do. Our greater focus is to end the cruelty on one property at a time. Jail time for a puppy mill operator means little to me. You don't address suffering with suffering. You don't address cruelty with cruelty. We need to put in place a system where cruelty can end. The only effective way to end that cruelty is a court mandate stating that abusers are no longer allowed to possess, care for, or "own" any animals ever again. That is what I seek.

Yes, some of the people I shut down are evil, loathsome creatures, but I care more about letting the justice system work than I do about any specific punishment or jail sentence. I'm not wishing hate on anyone. I'm trying to end the hate.

And then there is the chicken. On that day early in my career when I rescued chickens from a séance, I didn't fully understand the lives of far too many of these feathered animals. Today, there are hundreds of billions of chickens and eggs produced in America every year. Most of them are factory farmed. And while it may seem logical to assume that chickens tasked with laying eggs would have easier lives than chickens raised for meat, the sad truth is that egg-laying chickens are victims of a different set of horrors, starting on the day they hatch.

These peeping yellow balls of fluff are sent down a conveyor belt to be sexed by factory workers, and if found to be male, they are immediately disposed of because they can neither provide eggs nor be a valuable strain for meat. The most common methods of disposal are suffocation, maceration via a high-speed grinder, and electrocution by being vacuumed up into a "kill plate." For every male chick that does not make it past day one, there is a female chick that does. The United States had 346 million laying hens engaged in the commercial production of eggs, according to the last count in 2013 by the United States Department of Agriculture.

The vast majority of laying hens are housed in battery cages. Each cage contains five to ten laying hens, with each allocated sixty-seven square inches of floor space, about the size of a piece of letter-sized paper. The cages are stacked side by side, many tiers high, allowing for as many as 100,000 hens in a single building, without access to sunlight or fresh air. Cramped in these cages, the hens have no room to express their natural behaviors of perching, nesting, preening, dust-bathing, and foraging—let alone walking or spreading their wings. Unable to move, they develop severe osteo-porosis. This, in turn, leads to a high incidence of bone fracture.

Cage-free hens, as the name implies, are loose in a barn, but they, too, have no access to the outdoors. Density can be nearly as cramped as battery cages. This leaves the hens with slightly more space, but not enough to escape hens that now have enough room to engage in feather-pecking: repeatedly pecking at the feathers of another. This behavior is a method of redirecting frustrated foraging motivations onto each other. It signifies poor welfare and results in bodily injury and oftentimes cannibalism. Factory farm operators address the issue of feather-pecking by partially amputating hens' beaks when they are less than ten days old, using scissors, heated blades, infrared light, or electric currents—all without anesthetics. Chickens have highly sensitive receptors in the tips of their beaks that are their main source of tactile stimuli. This mutilation is acutely painful and chronically impairing.

Free-range systems are not much better. Hens are loose in the barn and are provided access to the outdoors; however, due to poor facility design and lack of regulation, many hens never actually go outside. The USDA simply requires that free-range animals have "access" to outdoor areas, but there is no provision for quality or quantity of time spent outside. Furthermore, these hens are subject to all of the same cruelties as other commercial laying hens, such as beak amputation and male infanticide.

Organic facilities do not fare much better in terms of welfare, simply adding a stipulation that the hens' diet be all vegetarian and organic and free of pesticides, antibiotics, and growth hormones.

After approximately eighteen months, hens are considered "spent." As their reproductive capabilities decline, they are "depopulated." Unlike broiler chickens, whose carcasses fetch value on the market, laying hens who are considered spent have no commercial value, post-mortem. With their bodies osteoporotic from lack of exercise and calcium depletion from eggshell formation, most processing plants won't even take them. Some farmers, instead of paying to transport the hens long distances to one of the few processing plants that will accept them, just slaughter the birds. Some pack living birds into containers and bulldoze them into the ground.

Each year, more than eight billion broiler chickens are killed for food in the United States. Genetically selected for accelerated growth, increased breast-meat yield, and decreased food conversion ratio, the most common strains now reach market at less than forty days of age. These birds suffer a surfeit of metabolic and locomotive disorders. They often develop ascites (a build-up of fluid in the peritoneal cavity, the space between the lining of the abdomen and abdominal organs) and sudden heart failure due to the extreme pressure put on their underdeveloped internal organs. They collapse under their own weight, as their little bones cannot keep up with their muscle development. Studies generally find that about a third of broilers are lame or completely non-ambulatory, their legs wrought with arthritis, ruptured tendons, microfractures, and deformities. As a result, these birds spend as much as 90 percent of their time sitting on soiled litter, developing lesions from ammonia burns.

Although most broiler chickens are slaughtered at a mere six weeks of age, a few are kept on for a year or two as breeders. The unnaturally rapid growth rate, while usually a desirable trait, poses challenges to the "long term" health and reproductive capabilities of these chickens. They are simply too sickly by the time they reach sexual maturity to be sufficiently productive, so the industry came up with a solution: starve them. Chronic food restriction decreases fat deposition, heart disease, skeletal disease, lameness, mortality, and food costs—while increasing fertility. From as early as one week of age, breeder chickens are kept in a chronic state of hunger, provided with only a quarter to a third of the food they would have eaten, had they been given free access. In order to "recycle" the hens for an additional year, food is altogether withdrawn from hens for seven to fourteen days to speed up the molting process and start a new cycle of egg-laying.

Male breeder chickens are additionally subject to a standard set of mutilations, including beak amputation, despurring, and declawing, in order to protect the female hens from their aggressive and often violent behavior during mating.

If their lives weren't sad enough already, many chickens are injured or killed while being transported to slaughter. Rough, manual catching appears to be the primary source of bone fracture. Hens may be exposed to temperature extremes and deprived of food and water for more than twenty-four hours during transit to the processing plant. Upon arrival at the plant, the chickens are strung upside down by their fragile legs in metal shackles and conveyed through an electrical water-bath stunner. Stunning prior to slaughter is practiced in order to induce unconsciousness and insensibility, as well as immobilization. A large number of problems exist with this practice: the potential for pre-stun electric shocks that induce painful tonic (convulsive) seizures while the chickens are still conscious; inadequate electrical frequencies that fail to induce unconsciousness or do so only momentarily because other frequencies may degrade meat quality; and the possibility of not making contact with the stunning apparatus at all.

After passing through the electrical water-bath stunner, an automated knife cuts the chickens' throats so that they bleed out, and then they are submerged in a tank of scalding hot water. Chickens that are inadequately stunned and cut enter the scald tank fully conscious.

In the United States, there are currently only two federal laws in place that govern the treatment of farmed animals: the 28-Hour Law, which covers animals during transport, and The Humane Methods of Livestock Slaughter Act, which covers animals during slaughter. They both exclude all species of poultry. And the federal Animal Welfare Act excludes farmed animals altogether. This means that chickens, which make up over 90 percent of all animals used in agriculture, have no federal protection. The suffering and cruelty they endure is legal.

Society is slowly coming to consider the conditions of all animals. To me, that is a moral imperative because all lives have value. I don't believe in a hierarchy of animals. In my rescue work, we show people how dogs—animals that have legal protections—are actually treated in puppy mills, and how animals that lack any significant legal protections, like chickens and other farmed animals, are treated as well.

We as a society need to put an end to places of suffering equally—puppy mills, dog fighting operations, factory farms, fur farms, circuses, research labs, and other industries that profit from animal suffering. Puppy mills are the gateway to exposing cruelty. Concern for animals that often are our companions can lead to greater concern for those we frequently call "livestock." When we eliminate puppy mills, I believe the dominoes of cruelty will begin to fall.

We are building an army of compassion through shutting down puppy mills, changing people's hearts and minds, and gradually showing them the reality of other forms of animal cruelty.

CHAPTER ELEVEN

TOOLS OF THE TRADE

Several times a year, Animal Rescue Corps puts on what we call BARC: our Basic Animal Rescue Course. It is an opportunity to train the people who will expand the cadre of volunteers we depend on, whether they become community liaisons, administrative assistants, scribes working with veterinarians on rescues, or the handlers who will take from my arms the animals I have just pulled from hellish places. But the BARC training is more than just an introduction to working with ARC; it is a weekend of immersion in humane education, an intense course in how to put concern for animals into practice. BARC provides a chance for committed individuals to meet, often for the first time, in an atmosphere of communal compassion.

BARC began as a one-day course. It is now spread over two days—one introductory, the second more detailed and highly strategic. On this late-summer weekend, we are in the small town of Lebanon, Tennessee, near Nashville, in the Capitol Theater, a classic, old-style movie theater converted for the weekend to an oversized classroom. The theater is owned—and donated for BARC—by Pam Black, a stalwart Tennessee Animal Rescue Corps supporter and volunteer on several rescue operations. Some in the group have traveled from as far as Rhode Island, Arizona, and California.

We show a lot of videos at BARC conferences, mostly documentary footage of ARC rescue actions: missions like Operation Unbridled Spirit, Operation Delta Dogs, and Operation Liberty Dogs. After each video, as the lights come up, tears and tissues are plentiful, and not just from the audience.

As the first speaker, I strive to be inspirational. "Thank you for bringing your compassion," I begin, reminding our partners of the privilege we share in giving animals the chance to reclaim their lives. We are in the business of saving lives, of removing animals from cages, striving to eliminate cages and chains. We create lasting solutions in communities. We make the promise to each and every one of those animals that we are going to save their lives.

As the founder of Animal Rescue Corps, I am most often the organization's public face—to donors, to volunteers, to elected officials, and to the news media. But BARC is about learning and sharing. The passion in the room for what we do is evident, but today is all about training, about how to accomplish important things. "If we don't have structure," I say, "we are operating on emotion." In a rescue operation, emotion must take a back seat to careful execution.

Over two days, we will discuss rescue operations, building a rescue team, the tools of animal rescue, animal behavior under stress, health conditions, legalities of animal rescue, rescuing a dog (or a child, for that matter) from a hot car, photographing rescued animals, and much more.

In this forum or any place I speak publicly, there are linguistic ground rules I insist on. I have already mentioned them on these pages, but they bear repeating. We don't refer to an animal as an "it" but as "him" or "her." Animals are not objects. Nor do we refer to people as "owners," because that word implies animals are property. I use the term "guardians."

Some of those assembled in the Tennessee theater have volunteered with ARC before. Others may wind up, at some point in the future, working on a rescue deployment. But any of the people in this BARC class could wind up attempting to rescue a lost or hurt animal on the side of a highway. In a puppy mill, I am almost always the one making initial contact with animals; in day-to-day life, the person making initial contact could be anyone. That is why we spend considerable time talking about how to get animals to safe places.

The first concerns on a rescue—of any scale—are logistical. I choose a capable team and keep it tight. We evaluate our surroundings and assess personal safety considerations, species-specific precautions, and animals' methods of defense. That could mean, in a puppy mill, that we wear gloves to help protect against bites, along with masks that protect our lungs against high levels of ammonia. In a primate rescue, the precautions necessary might include full-body protective suits, masks, and face shields. We secure loose animals first, eliminate exit routes for contained animals, and identify the entry and exit routes we will use to extract each of them. We evaluate each animal's condition and body language, although we strive not to use medical terms or behavioral labels—like "aggressive"—that may stick. These are animals under extreme stress in horrid conditions. At this point, labels do not help. We determine if each animal can be carried or if she must immediately be crated.

Process is important, but it is clear that the people in the seats before me most want to hear about the "how": How do you extract a petrified, damaged animal who does not know what a kind, gentle touch feels like?

I focus much of the discussion on dogs and cats, since they are the species we most often rescue, and I make clear that we must tailor our approach to each individual's behavior, physical condition, and environment.

My first principle of extracting a dog is to avoid eye contact. I speak softly to her, and I try to act nonchalant, not letting her know she has my full attention. The best choice is to use nothing but my hands, my soft voice, and a low-and-slow approach. The dog is going to let me know how far I can move in. I will try to get down to her level and never move straight toward her. If she seems curious, I gently extend my hand for her to come to me. If not, I have to create a plan. I must move slowly, establish the dog's personal space, her comfort zone. Patience matters greatly, for the dog's safety and mine.

Even in such stressful conditions, dogs very often can differentiate between "safe" and "unsafe." A soft voice, a non-threatening body posture, and the low-and-slow approach can be all it takes for a dog to come close, accept a gentle touch, and allow a lead to be slipped on. After that, I pick her up, transfer her to a handler, and begin the process to a new life. The extraction isn't always that easy, of course, and we have an escalating series of methods we can employ.

We employ the tools and tactics of animal rescue in the most humane, safe manner possible. Any tool—whether a hammer, a chef's tongs, or a lead for a dog—is useful only if used correctly. In untrained hands, any tool can be dangerous. In untrained hands, animal rescue tools can appear to be items of cruelty.

One of the tools I favor is a lead made of braided steel covered by flexible plastic. When I am trying to extract an unknown, possibly fractious dog, it holds a natural loop, which I can use as a little lasso to slip over his head. If he begins "gator rolling"—flopping onto his back, flailing, squirming, and flipping—I can safely keep the lead around him, knowing he is not going to be able to chew through it with any speed.

When extracting a dog, even one that might try to bite me or a handler, I will pick him up whenever possible. The lead I have on him will allow me to extend my left arm in front of me while cradling him on my right side and keeping the lead taut, thus preventing him from turning to bite me. Most times, kneeling next to him, lifting to support his body, and bringing him close to me will help keep him calm. He feels safe and I am protected. If he turns to me, attempting to bite, I can extend my arm so he cannot get to my face.

When I pick him up and he recognizes that nothing bad is happening to him, we begin to develop a relationship of trust. In the majority of cases, we can find that bond in just a few seconds. If I can, I will set him down and pet him for a few moments. At that point, we have sealed our relationship.

One of the other tools we occasionally use has a long, spotted history. In countless cartoons and illustrations that portray "dog-catchers" as sadistic, slovenly men in uniform, the dogcatchers carry poles with nets on the end, chasing recalcitrant dogs. In far too many other portrayals—real ones, not cartoons—you can find images of people using what are often called "catch poles" or "control poles": four-foot-long aluminum poles with a loop of plastic-encased braided metal lead on the end. With a quick Google search, you can find images of control poles being used like fishing rods, with a dog caught in the noose, or like a broom, with a dog snared in the lasso and shoved into a corner. Such uses of a control pole are as wrong as the pictures are inflammatory. For me, the control pole is a tool of necessity, in a potentially dangerous situation.

I use the control pole only to handle biting dogs. I slip the circle around a dog's neck. I tighten the loop—again, not to strangle, but to control. I secure the pole in my left hand, which gives me even more control of a strong dog, to make sure he can't get to my face. And it allows me to carry a fractious dog on my right side, since I am right-handed and have greater strength on my right. By carrying that dog I have the opportunity to establish a bond of trust by establishing control so that nothing negative happens to the dog. Used correctly and sparingly, even the control pole can be a tool of compassion.

I've used bolt cutters, too, in rescues. For dogs, one of the worst-case scenarios they endure is being forced to fight. One of the videos we show during BARC chronicles an operation called Delta Dogs in the tiny town of Isola, Mississippi. The video includes images of our team posing next to a pile of twisted, dirty chains and steel poles. Just a few hours before, each post and each chain held a fighting dog.

All of the dogfighting operations I have seen look remarkably similar. If you could view them from an aerial perspective, the first thing you would notice is circles. Fighting dogs are normally chained, each to a secure pole. The dogs run in circles at the end of their chains until they carve those shapes into the dirt. Those circles do not intersect but are so close together that dogs can almost touch each other. I've often wondered about the perverse kind of geometry that aligns these circles so perfectly.

A dogfighting operation most often has a sparring ring of some sort. In the etiquette of this sadistic activity, dogfights are rarely held on the property of a breeder, but dogs must practice fighting. Also, potential buyers of fighting dogs want to see them in action. There is usually a crude treadmill for training. You will also find a burn pile: a charred spot likely to contain dog remains. There will probably be a spring pole, a beam-like structure that suspends a target above the ground that a dog will leap to grab and hold onto, to build his strength.

This property had them all.

Dogfighting is such a vile activity that even to describe how it works is giving its criminal practitioners too much publicity, too much satisfaction. It is a practice utterly devoid of gray areas: It is entirely about cruelty, sadism, violence, and death.

Like all dogs, pit bulls are not inherently violent and make excellent, loving companion animals. But in the wrong hands, they, like most dogs, can be made to harm others. Distinguishing the dangerous from the potentially docile is often not terribly difficult. Most are not that way, and none of the dogs in this fighting operation posed a threat.

Getting the dogs to safety and a place of care and concern, however, was not easy. The operators of dogfighting operations are a generally paranoid lot. They worry about someone absconding with their meal tickets. That's why we found the dogs with tight-fitting, thick leather collars that had heavy padlocks connecting the dogs to heavy chains. The chains were, in turn, connected to steel poles buried deeply in the ground. In a stressful situation like this, virtually the only option my team and I have is to cut dogs free.

The operation is simple: I calm and hold the dog, and a team member uses a three-foot-long set of bolt cutters to snap the chain, several links away from the dog. It's an unmistakable sound: a loud click followed by the clunk of heavy chain links hitting the ground.

When it comes time to cut dogs free, members of the team want in. Each wants a turn, a chance to set an abused dog free, actually and metaphorically. Few of them talk at that moment. Most cry. The pictures end up, more often than not, as Facebook profile pictures—when the case is over and law enforcement has approved their use. They are moments of triumph. The video, shown at BARC, lets us all relive one of those moments.

Compassion shared.

CHAPTER TWELVE

A MONTH OF RACING
TO RESCUES

"I don't understand," she said, her voice choked with emotion, as tears began to flow, "how somebody could do this."

My team and I hear that sentiment often—from a volunteer or someone watching a video of one of our deployments. It is overwhelming to see for the first time—or every time, for that matter—the living, breathing embodiment of the cruelty people are capable of inflicting on animals.

These words, however, were spoken on this day by someone who has been with ARC on dozens of missions, someone who has, again and again, been in the first wave to enter those hell holes, documenting the awful places we walk into, recording in digital photographic pixels the crimes against animals we put an end to, along with the redemption we strive to offer. Amiee Stubbs is propelled by compassion, but she is also tough. She is able to look, without flinching, at scenes of horror and make images people remember. That this particular situation in Coffee County, Tennessee, so strongly affected Amiee speaks volumes about just how awful it was.

But it's also the middle of this story about a month—April 2015—that tested ARC's limits.

The story began months prior, with a tip about a breeding operation in the town of Saint Anne in Kankakee County, Illinois, about an hour south of Chicago. ARC had been contacted by a Chicago-based advocacy group called The Puppy Mill Project. They told us of a notorious local puppy mill that had been in existence for years despite multiple attempts to shut it down. A former employee of the puppy mill, we were told, might be able to get inside and gather evidence under the guise of shopping for a dog. We coached the former employee, who said she believed she could have a look at the place. We got a hidden camera and microphone on her. The effort failed. The puppy mill owner brought out a puppy to show, but would not allow the former employee in any area where a large number of dogs were housed. A subsequent attempt by a local group also failed to gain sufficient evidence to take prompt action.

We at ARC did our own research and found that animal control in the area had been trying for years to shut the place down, but had been blocked by state agricultural officials who made cursory inspections and passed the facility. We approached Julie Boudreau, director of the Kankakee County Animal Control and Adoption Center, and offered our assistance. She promised to get back to us, if a case ever came together.

In the meantime, a number of concerned groups appeared before a Kankakee County board committee, urging action. This, of course, is not the situation we prefer. Publicity when we are trying to conduct an investigation does not help. But in this case, it led to an unexpected, and positive, outcome.

In a March 2014 interview for an article about the board meeting, the *Daily Journal* of Kankakee reported Boudreau "said she has been asking the state to inspect the St. Anne business with greater scrutiny since 2006. She said the state has too few investigators, who are often overworked."

After the meeting and the story, Boudreau heard from the state's attorney, who wanted to get involved. Boudreau called ARC. We began to plan for action, despite some lingering concerns, largely on my part, about how officials would obtain a search warrant without fresh evidence.

About a week out, we got a major break. We received word from a local source that the puppy mill had released several dogs to a local rescue group—as puppy mills sometimes do when breeding dogs can no longer breed. Boudreau jumped on the case, intercepted the dogs, and persuaded the rescue group to turn them over. We had our Chicago liaison pick them up and take them to our Chicago-based veterinarian, who wrote a report about their compromised health, urging the confiscation of all dogs from the facility.

The day of the raid—which we named Operation Spring Break—the sheriff's department and animal control went inside the house and served the warrant, as the veterinarian and I waited outside. I was invited in to talk to the puppy mill operator. I asked her to sign over the animals, and she did.

As with all puppy mills, there were sick and injured animals with eye infections, respiratory conditions, and dental issues living in high levels of ammonia. Although the dogs had been surrendered, they became evidence for a potential criminal case. Assessing their medical conditions took several days, with every toenail and clump of fur bagged and catalogued. Then ARC's animal behavior specialist came in to start assessing the behavior of the eighty dogs, which, as the sign outside the puppy mill indicated, were mainly Chihuahuas, Yorkshire Terriers, Shih Tzus, and Poodles.

There was one puppy who received an inordinate amount of attention. He was sickly, having been born with health issues. He went from hotel room to hotel room, as members of our team took turns staying up all night caring for him. A lot of energy went into saving his life, but he died several weeks later, despite their selfless efforts.

At the end of the fifth day of Operation Spring Break, just as we were wrapping up for the evening to head back to the hotel, we received some startling news. Kim Rezac approached me and said, "Scotlund, I've got something here. Something's brewing in the Nashville area. The sheriff is on scene of what sounds like a puppy mill. I'm waiting for more information."

Kim is someone I listen to about situations we need to pursue. A business owner, founder of her own foster-based rescue organization, ARC liaison, wife of a police officer, and mother of two young-adult women, Kim manages an incredible number of life tasks and never seems to push anything to the back burner. Soft-spoken and never showing signs of stress in tough situations, she is in charge of medical management for ARC's operations. Animal rescue is something of a family passion. Kim's daughter Lindsey Rezac is one of our primary undercover investigators and has been responsible for generating dozens of ARC's cases.

Kim was getting reports from various individuals that something was occurring, something urgent and dire, but we didn't know what. However, when law enforcement reaches out to us, especially if a sheriff is already at the site of a cruelty case, we go into high alert. Rather than relying on reports, I asked Kim to get us in touch directly with the detective on the scene. He returned the call just as we were climbing into our vehicles. As I was finishing the conversation, I signaled the other vehicles in our group to stay put and asked that other members of the team who had already headed for the hotel to come back immediately. The sheriff had briefly described the situation, and he sent a single photograph—a picture of an extremely matted, filthy, sickly terrier mix in an even filthier cage, her head hanging low and her eyes utterly vacant. The filth, the body posture, and her eyes made it clear we had a difficult choice to make: stay in place and finish our current operation or split up. We were in the midst of a deployment, but this was a desperate case. The entire team piled into ARC's mobile command post and discussed the possibility that, for the first time, we might have to divide into two teams hundreds of miles apart. Because my already exhausted team members would have to make even greater sacrifices, I knew this had to be a team decision.

The sheriff had agreed, for the time being, not to go to the media or otherwise announce that anything was happening. A deputy would secure the property overnight. We did not know the number of dogs affected or just how bad all of the conditions were.

"Are you prepared to drive all night, a nine or ten hour drive, and then go streaming straight into hell first thing in the morning?" I asked. We talked about what we had and what was in front of us, and I shared the one picture we were given. There was no hesitation. Every team member said we needed to act in the best interest of both sets of animals.

We had never contemplated such a decision before: that Animal Rescue Corps would run two major operations at one time. We had no emergency shelter for the new raid. We had a partial team that was already running on fumes. We had no equipment gathered. Between seven in the evening, when we decided to go, and midnight, when we hit the road, we planned it. People organized. People loaded trucks. People mobilized volunteers on the other end. I have never seen such a well-synchronized operation.

Our caravan hit the road. I left the driving to others, in no small part because I had a new operation—now named Operation Midnight Run—for which I needed to find financial donors. I worked for a couple hours, slept for a couple, and went back to work. By the time we arrived, I had at least the initial funds committed for the rescue.

During the trip, one of our team members driving the rescue rig hit and killed a coyote. The animal had run across the street and hit the step on the vehicle's side. The driver was a mess. The incident was unavoidable, but as a person of compassion for all animals, he was riddled with guilt and remorse. I woke up during a stop for gas and found him hosing off blood and bits of the animal. I had to give him a pep talk.

We drove straight from Kankakee County to the sheriff's office in Coffee County, Tennessee, about sixty-five miles southeast of Nashville. We met with the sheriff. Knowing that the facility had been secured and the sheriff had the paperwork done, we left his office, headed to the property, and walked into pure hell.

The property sat down a long country road past a bunch of spacious country houses surrounded by lush grass already brilliant green in April. The property owner's house occupied just a small section of her property, with a barn and some other structures visible from the driveway. The sheriff was eager to go. We grabbed respirator masks, after a local hazardous materials official sampled the ammonia levels and determined that masks were sufficient, and the sheriff gave our small exploration team—myself, Amy Haverstick, Kim, and our veterinarians on the case, Dr. Edwards and Dr. Jones—a tour. It started bad and got worse. There were dogs stacked in cages in various rooms of the house. The carpet was saturated with urine that, in some rooms, formed puddles. Dogs were stacked in the living room, just feet from a table with a lit candle on it. There were pictures on the wall, a seemingly normal living room alongside crevices of horror.

Behind her house were the structures holding most of the animals. We stopped briefly in the driveway to get our bearings, and then walked through the barn, into the yard, and around a corner, where we found the outbuilding we look for and dread finding on every puppy mill case.

From our initial assessment, we knew that on a scale of one to ten, this was a ten. What we confronted were not just captive, mistreated dogs; they were statues. They were alive, yes, but most didn't move from the backs of their cages, didn't return a glance, didn't respond to a gentle voice. They had given themselves over to death. It's something I have seen before but never get used to. Every dog we found was sullen, existing in his or her own waste, with high levels of ammonia and no food or water.

The horror we confronted, coupled with sleep deprivation, hit us hard. Amiee broke down. I did, too. I walked away from the others and called Tim Woodward, who was not on site, as he and Karla were in charge of finishing up the Kankakee case, to brief him on the situation. As I walked him through the scenes we had just witnessed, I lost my composure, forgetting in the moment that our videographer had a wireless microphone on me and heard everything.

In addition to dogs who had succumbed to death but were still alive, we found a number of bodies; six of them had been tossed into a wheelbarrow with a filthy blanket thrown over top. Four others had perished in their disgusting cages, and their bodies remained there, with living animals next to them.

Despite the dogs' stillness, the bars of their cages appeared to be in constant motion, as years of accumulated fur, dust, and dander flitted in what little breeze there was. Seemingly every surface we encountered had the same coating: rough-hewn walls, crude floors, and joists above that were the closest things to ceilings. Mounds of accumulated feces lined the floors of every enclosure. At least a dozen cages with animals in them were rusted shut. Although they weren't padlocked, I had to break my way in, which indicated that those dogs had never been out of their cages. Many dogs had festering, untreated skin infections and a coating of fleas. Many had difficult-to-look-at eye conditions. We found one dog with a prolapsed uterus and raced her to emergency treatment. All long-coated dogs were covered with mats and feces over at least 80 percent of their bodies. One dog I found didn't move at all when I went to get him. A scan with my flashlight made it all too sickeningly clear: His feces-caked, matted fur had gotten snagged on the cage and, over time, his fur had grown into the bars of the cage. I had to cut him free.

I took a break midway through the job of removing dogs from the house to allow the intake and evidence teams to catch up. As I walked past the row of handlers waiting for their dogs to be examined, I saw something I'd never seen before: Every dog had his or her nose pointed toward the sky. These dogs had not been out of the darkness for weeks and months, if not years; they might never have taken a breath of fresh air, and they were savoring every moment in the sun.

Near sundown, I handed off the last dog to Dan Stubbs. In all, we removed eighty-five dogs and several cats. Our team at the emergency shelter raced to provide them veterinary care, likely for the first time.

It was clear that this was a hoarding situation. But was it a puppy mill? We found mostly small, pure-bred dogs like those we see during puppy mill cases. But most of the dogs were older, possibly past breeding age. There was no sign outside advertising puppies for sale. We could find no website, Facebook page, or any other indication that this person was breeding or selling the dogs. But every one appeared to have been a puppy mill dog. Had she operated a puppy mill years ago and stopped? She said no, and there was no evidence of a business on the premises. My strong suspicion is that puppy mill operators looking to get rid of spent dogs gave them to her. Why she kept all of the dogs is something of a mystery. It wasn't for commerce and was likely a case of hoarding. They went from existing in a puppy mill, breeding until they could no longer breed, to living out their lives starving and dehydrated in this shithole, without the most basic of care.

We set up our emergency shelter in a portion of a former Toshiba plant just outside of Nashville. A day or two later, we got a call from the Lebanon public health and safety department, which oversees animal control. The department had people on the scene of a case of starving and neglected dogs, most living on chains, and they asked us to come out. We mobilized and were there within half an hour of the call.

The area was what had once evidently been a campground, but was now a squatters' trailer park. Several dogs had been found in a severely rundown camper, a filth-encrusted trailer that was clearly someone's home. The animal control officer had already removed those dogs. The rest were chained outside. During our work, an eleven-year-old girl wearing fraying cut-off pants and a ratty t-shirt watched us. She lived in the camper. This was a family that had virtually nothing to their names. Although we shot pictures and video of the rescue, we didn't show the camper, for fear of bringing public shame to the girl.

"Shouldn't she be in school?" I asked the official in charge.

"Yes, she should be," he replied.

"Well, why isn't she?"

"They're homeschooling her."

"Do you believe that?"

"No," he answered. "They would never be approved for a home school."

"Have you called Child Protective Services?"

"We have. They said they wouldn't respond."

I told him that I believed the child was living in conditions as bad as the animals were, and that we at ARC would go on record with Child Protective Services, the media, or anyone else necessary.

The sheriff promised to renew his call to Child Protective Services. When we submitted our report, knowing that it would go to the district attorney, we focused several paragraphs on the child and her living conditions.

During the course of a rescue, it isn't uncommon for team members—both staff and volunteers—to become enamored with certain animals. Never, though, is anyone allowed to adopt a dog on the spot. ARC doesn't adopt out dogs; our placement partners do, and that is the sole route to adopting a dog we have rescued.

On a rescue, I normally do not find the time to form a special bond with any animal. I am too busy looking after all to fall in love with one. But, in its own unique way, our three-destination odyssey that began in Kankakee led to a special relationship with Chicago.

After the seizure in Kankakee, Julie Boudreau, the animal control officer, invited us to see her facility. On the tour, the last dog we came across was in a dark corner, but I caught a glimpse of his eyes. As I got closer, I could see his tail wagging. He licked my hand. A big dog, Boudreau told us he had been picked up as a stray about a week before. She offered me a closer look. He came out and showed off. He was goofy and happy, greeting each person. It's probably fair to say I was smitten with the big dog.

I told Boudreau I was interested and would think about him. I called her the next day to ask if I could visit him again. Instead, she brought him to me at our emergency shelter. The day lasted into night. I called my family. We named him Chicago.

Had I not chosen to adopt him, Chicago would have come with us anyway. When ARC works with community officials, we often take a large number of the animals, if not all, from the local shelter to our emergency shelter and work with our placement partners to find homes for them, in addition to the animals we removed from the case. In the case of Chicago, a mix of Rotweiller, pit bull, and mastiff, who now tips the scales at more than one hundred pounds, we were fortunate to find each other. Chicago is the latest beloved member of the Haisley family, and he has spent most of his time during the writing of this book where he is now, with his enormous head on my lap.

Finding Chicago was a capstone to a unique month.

CHAPTER THIRTEEN

AMERICA'S SHELTERS

In my time in animal protection, I have witnessed progress in the way society treats and addresses animals, specifically in the area of animal sheltering. I have been on the front lines of some of it. Society's attitudes toward animals are changing, for the better. But to truly make lasting change, we need to honestly assess where we are.

The practice of "impounding" animals or bringing them to a "pound" began in the United States in the seventeenth century. In the American colonies, livestock found wandering was taken to animal pounds, where individuals claiming "ownership" could reclaim their animals for a fee. Later, "stray" dogs and cats were included in the pound system, but because they had little or no monetary value, they were typically put to death within days.

In 1869, Philadelphia philanthropist Caroline Earle White created America's first "humane animal shelter," and in 1912, an organization she founded, the Women's Humane Society, introduced the first known animal adoption program. Other humane organizations in other communities quickly followed. By the 1870s, many states had animal protection laws and humane organizations to help enforce them. The 1880s saw the spread of effective humane education programs.

A cornerstone of modern animal sheltering is sterilization: spaying and neutering of dogs and cats to prevent unwanted litters. Veterinarians in the 1930s and 1940s began to practice the procedures, but they were far from perfect—risky and painful, and according to some at the time, inhumane. Los Angeles introduced the first public spay and neuter clinic in 1969, a move that demonstrated a newfound level of public acceptance for surgeries that are commonplace today.

When I started my career, the generally accepted figure of how many animals were put to death in American shelters each year was twenty million. Today, thanks in no small part to an increase in animal adoptions, coupled with spay and neuter programs, that estimated number is often cited at a little under three million.

There are more than 5,000 animal shelters and perhaps twice as many independent rescue or foster groups throughout the nation. In the best cases, animal shelters are positive and influential animal welfare centers of their communities, operating at the highest of standards. They accept unwanted and unclaimed pets, medically treat and sterilize all of their inhabitants, provide rehabilitation, training, and enrichment programs to all who enter, and successfully place all healthy animals directly in new homes or with placement partners. In addition, many of the best shelters offer effective programs outside their facility walls, such as free to low-cost spay and neuter procedures, vaccinations, micro-chipping, humane education programs, foster networking, humane law enforcement, and animal care and control services. These are the best cases, and a standard we must work toward in every community.

While our country has made tremendous progress for animals in the last century and a half, we are, unfortunately, still a society in which not all life is thought to have value. Many still consider animals to be disposable commodities. Some cash-strapped communities offer few or no animal welfare services. Most communities lack preventive programs, such as humane education, training, and affordable spay and neuter services. Problems within existing shelters include mismanagement, lackluster or poorly run adoption programs, transfer programs without proper oversight, insufficient funds to operate at an adequate level of care, buildings lacking the proper design, and deteriorating facilities. These deficiencies result in millions of companion animals, exotics, and wildlife entering a sheltering system rife with what should be unacceptable conditions, resulting in healthy animals needlessly being put to death.

I believe we must stop at nothing until our communities and all of our animal shelters have achieved best-case scenarios. This is the new standard we must achieve in the second century of animal sheltering. I recognize, as everyone must, that many shelters do not have the resources to immediately establish the highest standards of facility design, operations, and animal care, but I believe, with community support, every shelter can make at least incremental, and sometimes profound, progress toward enhanced standards. As individual communities and a nation, we must progress.

We are placing animals into an environment that is as unnatural as it can get, and they are going to decline in all areas: physically, emotionally, and socially. Our mission and our facilities are still too often at odds with each other. The solution to fixing our system of animal sheltering has to include every possible option. In any shelter environment, you need to approach problems from every angle: the highest standards of operation, a solid philosophy, effective policies, procedures that work, solution-based programs, and a facility that meets the basic and more complicated needs of all of its inhabitants.

The shelter, after all, is not a single thing; shelters are a range of facilities. Shelters evolve from being pounds. Pounds are "catch-and-kill facilities." Pounds bring in animals, but there is no real initiative to get them adopted, unless outside, private rescue organizations become involved. Some animal "catch-and-kill" facilities have attempted to become adoption centers, with varying levels of success. There really is no such thing as a minimum standard of care recognized by law, other than adequate shelter, food, water, and veterinary care. How far shelters evolve depends on leadership driven by true compassion and a belief that improvement is a continual process.

The first principle I believe we must work toward is genuinely understanding and accurately compiling statistics. As a society, we must be honest about our problems in order to fix them. We truly don't know how many animals are put to death each year in shelters because we have long lacked standard reporting methods. Nor do we know the reasons why those animals are put to death because such information has rarely been part of standard record keeping. Without that information, the "why," it is exceptionally difficult to understand how we are going to change our sheltering system. We need to know the causes in order to determine the changes that can be made to give every homeless animal the opportunity to live as a loved member of a family.

In their record keeping, most shelters differentiate between "healthy destroyed" versus "problem destroyed," without any additional nuance. Healthy destroyed is fairly simple to explain: reasons include space, color, and breed. Overcrowded shelters often deal with space constraints irresponsibly by putting animals to death. Problem destroyed is more complicated. If a dog has, say, lymphosarcoma, rare is the shelter that can afford—or raise funds for—treatment. Even the best-funded shelters are unlikely to have the resources to take multiple dogs through a regimen of chemotherapy. But many shelters will say that a cat with an upper respiratory infection or a dog with kennel cough is "problem destroyed" because of infectious disease. Yet with proper protocols and facilities, those conditions are treatable and manageable.

The closest thing we have to a reporting standard in shelters today originated in 2004, when a group of animal welfare leaders from twenty one organizations came together under a mission of saving more healthy and treatable companion animals. Importantly, the group did not seek to condemn some shelters and support others; they worked to understand difficult situations. The conferees' guiding principles state, "We acknowledge that the euthanasia of healthy and treatable animals is the sad responsibility of some animal welfare organizations that neither desired nor sought this task." Even though the term euthanasia was once again incorrectly assigned and I don't accept the phrase "sad responsibility," I support the effort being made. This recognition—that municipal animal shelters have to confront difficult choices—is vital to making change.

The groups developed what are known as the Asilomar Accords, which defined terms used to describe health and condition: healthy, treatable, rehabilitatable, manageable, unhealthy, and untreatable. The Asilomar Accords also provided statistical reporting methods for intake, adoptions, treatment, and euthanasia. The group developed formulas and forms for reporting information on all of the categories listed above. While not ubiquitous in the field, efforts like this are a worthy start toward standard reporting practices—from municipal shelters and private shelters alike.

Once we understand why animals are put to death in shelters, we can make more responsible decisions and begin to find ways to save more of those lives. So my second principle of improvement in sheltering is that putting a shelter animal to death should be justified and not be a simple black-and-white decision. There should be a process, a series of steps taken prior to an irrevocable choice. Is a dog showing aggression toward other dogs? There are behavioral interventions that may help. Is the dog showing aggression toward humans? There are steps to be taken for these concerns as well. Is the dog black and not the more traditionally desirable yellow? Is a cat feral? Is a cat sneezing? Is the animal sick? Is he contagious? Is a cat pregnant? None of these, I would argue, is an automatic reason for putting an animal to death. Some behaviors can be resolved. Some dogs and cats can be treated. Some situations can be changed. Certainly not all, but many.

Assessments are important, about more than just physical condition. Animal shelters only recently began assessing animals using facts about temperament and behavior.

One of the pioneers in the movement toward shelter assessments is Sue Sternberg, who developed a protocol called Assess-A-Pet. (Sue has been a friend since 1995 when I first met her in New York City and asked her to help me put together an assessment program for the Manhattan shelter.) Assess-A-Pet uses a temperament assessment to help shelters determine the appropriate course of action for each individual dog. It is a snapshot of where he is now, both in behavior and personality, and of the steps needed to be taken to correct any concerns. Is the undesired characteristic medically based or solely behavioral? Is it environmental or situational? What can the shelter do to correct or modify the issue? What enrichment program can we use for this dog? Does he need to work with a trainer who specializes in this sort of problem? Is he dangerous to staff or too dangerous to adopt out? If so, can the problem be corrected? Or is a foster home the best environment for this dog at this time?

By gathering data to assess the temperament of each dog, Assess-A-Pet took away less valuable characterizations, like how long a dog had been in a shelter, his breed, age, or physical imperfections. Assess-a-Pet and other scientifically validated programs have helped make it possible for shelter workers and volunteers to interact more safely with dogs and cats and to provide potential adopters with better descriptions of temperament. Such data-driven programs help us move away from assessments based on human traits and look at each animal as an individual—for who she is, based on observable behavior.

Another service, provided to shelters by the American Society for the Prevention of Cruelty to Animals, is Meet Your Match: an assessment tool that helps shelters rate dogs and cats in terms of friendliness, sociability, playfulness, energy level, ability to focus, motivations (food, people, or toys, for example), and "people manners." The evaluator uses the scores from the dog or cat's assessment to assign each animal a color (orange, green, or purple), which represents the levels of training and attention each animal is likely to need. Potential adopters then fill out a short questionnaire with categories that correspond to the categories on the animal's assessment. Adopters are then assigned a Meet Your Match color to match a dog's color: "Green adopters are most successful with dogs who like to be physically and mentally engaged; orange adopters are a good fit with middle-of-the-road dogs who are responsive and like regular activity and interaction; purple adopters are comfortable with dogs who have a laidback attitude and enjoy an easygoing lifestyle."

Through the Meet Your Match assessment, which is based on fact and observation, the ASPCA is helping local shelters achieve higher standards.

In 2005 I learned of a burgeoning program similar to dog assessments, but for cats. I knew this would be a long-awaited game changer for the way the sheltering community deals with cats. Needless to say, I couldn't wait to see it with my own eyes. The Humane Society of Boulder County, Colorado, was among the first animal shelters to introduce the Feline-ality assessments in 2006, and I jumped on the first plane I could to witness the future of animal sheltering for cats. Feline-ality was created by Emily Weiss, PhD, in conjunction with the ASPCA. Feline-ality is a reliable research based program that, through several steps, allows the assessor to predict cat behavior and personalities prior to going into an adoptive home. The program met my expectations and more. I was blown away.

This program worked, and it confirmed that the sheltering world knew very little about cat behavior and that we had been misidentifying cats' true behavior and personality traits. I, of course, immediately introduced the program at WARL.

Indeed, cats are no small part of the shelter equation. In fact, the plight of homeless cats is something of an elephant in the room of animal rescue and sheltering. We seem to consider and value them differently than dogs. While the rescue community continues to make steady, incremental progress in dealing with homeless dog issues, we have not seen the same kind of progress for cats, despite the dedicated work of a number of cat-focused groups and the introduction of the concept of Trap-Neuter-Return, or TNR, to the United States in 1980.

TNR is the practice of trapping, sterilizing, medically treating, and returning community (or feral) cats to where they were trapped. The best of these programs adds the additional component of "management," where the cat colony is monitored for health and environmental issues, provided supplemental food and shelter if needed, and where new additions to the colony are quickly trapped and neutered. These types of programs exist in many communities, sometimes created and operated informally by volunteers and other times by shelters or animal control departments within the community. Ideally, the operation of the program is legalized and codified by the adoption of a local ordinance to regulate the circumstances and procedures under which the cats are humanely trapped and returned as a means of controlling the community cat population. It is a compassionate alternative to putting healthy animals to death.

The scope of the problem is difficult to grasp because there is simply no accurate figure for the homeless cat population in this country. Estimates vary widely from 60 million to 100 million. Cats can populate at an astonishing rate. An unspayed female cat, her mate, and all of their offspring, producing two litters per year, with just under three surviving kittens per litter, can add up to more than eleven million cats in nine years. One irresponsible guardian failing to spay or neuter a cat can create an unmanageable environment and demonstrate that any solution that doesn't include sterilization as a primary component is doomed to fail.

While a cat's life on the street is not an easy one and TNR alone cannot provide all the solutions, sheltering is also a difficult proposition. Approximately 70 percent of cats are put to death in shelters each year, largely, shelters cite, because of a lack of adopters and space, old age, and spread of disease.

Additionally, resources like rescue and foster networks that exist for dogs outside of traditional shelters simply do not exist to the same degree for cats. There are fewer rescues that pull cats from shelters, and the few that are focused on this effort are typically filled to the brim with cats.

I encourage local animal protection advocates to push for a TNR ordinance and to contact elected officials, and I provide them with sample language for ordinances. I support groups teaming up with others who are working toward the same goal, to advocate progressive actions for cats and inspire others to get involved.

The stresses of living in a shelter lead to decline. Consequently, I firmly believe, as a third principle, that a key role for an animal shelter should be to pair animals with appropriate foster homes, to encourage a safe and comfortable environment in which foster families, fully briefed on an animal's status and assessment, can help continue the dog or cat's rehabilitation and ultimately pass along that information to an adopter.

Importantly, foster homes should be attached to a responsible organization with a network of temporary homes. Foster homes must not be warehouses for animals; putting a dog in a cage defeats the process.

Education is a vital part of the process of improving sheltering and fostering. In addition to large-scale animal rescues and humane education programs like our Basic Animal Rescue Course, Animal Rescue Corps works to improve animal sheltering in communities across the United States and beyond.

Along with proposing principles for improving shelters, I also conduct shelter assessments. Just as each animal is an individual, I realize each shelter is an individual, as well. So, too, is every shelter assessment. It's all about what works for that animal, that organization, and that community. Every case is different, but principle number four is that shelters must be evaluated frequently and comprehensively.

I don't use boilerplate standards when I assess a shelter. I look at how they function in their community, how they can improve for their community, and the role the community itself can play in creating a higher standard of operation. That is the endgame: to operate at the highest possible standards, within budgetary restraints; to not put to death any healthy or even potentially healthy animals; and to ultimately put itself out of business. It's about where they are now, where they can be tomorrow, and where they can be five or ten years from now.

The shelter assessments we do at ARC are often funded by individuals or foundations within communities, by people who hope to see shelter situations improve. Ultimately, I would love to have a partnership with a major corporation that would pay for a certain number of shelter assessments each year so groups could apply to be an evaluation-receiving shelter, having already lined up community support.

I spend a few days meeting with shelter leadership and municipal officials who oversee the shelter. There are tours to be taken and processes, policies, procedures, and philosophies to evaluate, along with volunteers and caretakers to meet. But then I spend days meeting with community stakeholders: partners of the shelter, rescue groups, organizations that take animals from the shelter, and non-profit support groups. I get everyone's input. I realize that a failing shelter is the product of the community and its government, and only the community can really fix those problems.

After a fact-finding trip, my team and I return to home base and develop a report that identifies the problems and suggests solutions that we present in person in a series of meetings. Sometimes we urge changes in leadership. In almost all cases, we push for shelters to get specific about what they do and why.

Regardless of a shelter's philosophies, policies, programs, and standard operating procedures, I believe it is essential, as principle number five, that those things be recorded. Sadly, the overwhelming majority of the shelters I evaluate have no written guiding principles. To me, that's insane. It's your foundation.

I ask, "What is your mission statement? What is your mission to your community, and what is your mission to your animals?"

Any shelter's mission should be to take in and care for animals—and to provide them rehabilitation, socialization, adoption, and an opportunity for those that have been lost to be reclaimed. But even though you may believe and mean those things, they are meaningless unless you have systems and written policies in place. No-cost programs like Meet Your Match and ASPCA's Safety Assessment for Evaluating Rehoming (SAFER) are great places to start.

Communities, in addition to shelters, need to consider their philosophies about animals as well. Some of those communities, where animals are not valued as they should be, might consider operations like the Rescue Waggin' program from PetSmart Charities, which takes animals from rural communities and transports them to shelters that do not have an abundance of animals.

Our challenges are not found only in rural communities with limited resources. Consider New York City. I have never seen such a high proportion of purebred dogs in what is otherwise perhaps America's most accepting, progressive city. I've never seen so many people wearing fur. I've never seen so many dogs that have not been spayed or neutered. Too many dogs that end up in shelters in New York—and scores of other large cities—were acquired as accessories, not as companions.

In addition to incremental improvements shelters could make today, there are systemic changes I believe we must work toward in all sheltering for the future.

First, if all animal guardianship required licensing, as we discussed earlier, it would demonstrate—on behalf of the community and on behalf of the animal—that guardianship is a significant responsibility. We could elevate guardianship to an earned privilege. People would have to prove their preparation for the responsibility, and they would take the decision to get a companion more seriously, because they would be held accountable for that choice.

Guardian licensing legislation wording and implementation would need to be tailored for each community, just as there are differences in animal control and sheltering systems across the country. The entities that would be charged with overseeing a law must be behind it, have an implementation plan in place, and be prepared for its outcomes if it is to be successful. If communities are not supportive or prepared, guardian licensing should not be enacted. If applied responsibly, guardian licensing would not only keep communities safe but also offer a community more than just an alternative to breed-specific legislation. It would provide a way to directly and proactively address irresponsible guardianship, which many humane societies, SPCAs, and shelters are already doing with adoption requirements. It is time to expand these ideas to society as a whole.

Second, I have long had a vision, which began when I was at the Washington Animal Rescue League, to create a national sheltering organization that could forge alliances with other groups, to build physical structures, philosophies, policies, protocols, and programs. Ultimately, my vision is to build as many as a dozen animal rescue leagues throughout the country, under unified management, with an internal transportation and transfer program, a network that could absorb regional problems and move animals in a practical, realistic, and safe manner to communities where their chances for adoption would skyrocket. My strategy would be to identify existing organizations that had the resources or the leadership to become part of this structure, until ultimately the entire network could be administered by one organization. In my vision, we would divide the country into as many as twelve regions. Each of our shelters would be the hub of a region. We would utilize our own program to get animals to the right places, all of which operated under the right philosophy. I looked at companies like FedEx and Southwest Airlines as prototypes of organization and data handling.

Third, I hope we see a day when we no longer need animal shelters primarily to house homeless animals. The best way to help homeless animals, to set them up for success in an adoptive family, is through temporary homes. Shelters, though, would still have considerable work to do. They would need to document lost animals, regardless of where they are housed and, in many cases, house them for the period of time most states require a stray dog or cat be held, which ranges from three to ten days. They would need to make behavior and medical assessments to look for immediate health concerns and ascertain whether animals need to be spayed or neutered, vaccinated, and microchipped. They would also need to treat illnesses and assess temperament, trying to identify the best placement option for that animal. And finally, they would still need to bear responsibility for providing food, toys, and enrichment items, and the financial commitments of medical or behavioral concerns.

We show our compassion by how we act and how we plan.

CHAPTER FOURTEEN

FAMILY

The day I started work at the Washington Animal Rescue League, virtually no one was expecting me. None of my interviews for the position had happened at the shelter. I was already familiar with the facility, and the board kept its interviews and deliberations confidential. The staff had been told a new boss was starting, their first executive director. I walked in, accompanied by Capone, and introduced myself. The two women at the front desk began calling people out of their offices and making introductions. In the increasingly crowded lobby, I particularly noticed the director of outreach. I was immediately smitten. So, apparently, was she. We kept our whirlwind relationship so quiet that the board didn't know we were a couple until we became engaged four months later. I proposed during a quiet dinner just before the opening of my art show at a local coffee house. As I dropped to one knee to propose, with Elvis Presley's recording of "Blue Christmas" playing in the background, I got an assist from the restaurant owner, who delivered a bouquet of flowers for me. A year later we got married, and a year after that we had our first daughter.

Perhaps because of my own upbringing, I am acutely aware of the challenges and pitfalls of the world my kids inhabit, and I hold them tight, knowing the time will come when I will have to trust them to make wise choices. I also see that there are parallels between my jobs as parent and animal rescuer. As you have already heard me say, terminology matters to me. "No," "don't," "can't," "shouldn't," and "impossible" make the list. One we have particularly taught our children to avoid is "hate." Hate is off limits. It represents everything we don't want our family to be. It's one word you won't hear me use. I want my family to be respectful, understanding, and compassionate. There is no place in that list for hate. It is what breaks us down, what separates us. So I sat my kids down for a talk. I went through a list of curse words—using the words, not abbreviations. I told them they are words we really shouldn't use, but if they do, I will gently remind them it's better not to. Hate, on the other hand, I told them, will earn them a talking to. They understand. They get the message. My son, however, took me at my word when I said I wouldn't punish them for cuss words.

Recently, in a conversation with my elder daughter, I used the word "Nazi." She asked me what the word meant. "Have they not yet covered Hitler or World War II or Anne Frank or the Holocaust in school?" I asked. Her answer was no. And with that, I launched into a half-hour story about World War II. I am no historian, but I walked her through the story, choosing my words and themes carefully. I told her the story of Hitler and war, of countries coming together to confront evil.

As we were finishing, my son, who is early in his elementary school years and had obviously been listening from another room, jumped in and started asking questions.

I knew he was too young to understand the nuances of the story I had just told his sister. I needed to figure out something age appropriate—some metaphor I could use to describe so much evil and suffering. Fortunately, the answer was draped over a chair in front of me: the "uniform" my son likes to wear, of Captain America, my childhood hero.

I referred to the first Captain America movie my son treasured, and the villain Red Skull, who was originally a Nazi agent in comic books. Captain America's troops were a metaphor for the Axis powers: former prisoners of war from different countries he recruited to fight the Nazis. I used Red Skull and Captain America's troops to metaphorically explain World War II. My son was transfixed.

When I concluded, I said, "The story I just told you is a true story."

He said, "So Captain America is real?"

I replied, "The spirit of Captain America is very, very real."

He thought for a moment, looked up at me and said, "*Yes!*"

On that evening, my childhood and his childhood had come together in a way I will explain to him someday. My wife already understood, and had tears streaming down her cheeks as she watched him. That was a beautiful and indelible moment in my life.

Moments like that can be fleeting in any family, and our family life is anything but typical. My work is clearly not a nine-to-five job. It isn't uncommon that I have to dive into a crisis, dropping everything else I'm doing to go rescue animals. And while I sometimes have to deploy on just a few hours' notice, exactly when the ARC team will finish its work—days, weeks, or months later—and we can return home is not clear usually until the very end of the rescue. I am away from home more than half the time. I recognize that when I am away, there are still children to care for, doctors' appointments, school meetings, illnesses, report cards, chores, and dozens of other responsibilities that all fall to my wife. Without a doubt, my work takes a toll on her. She handles burdens that are both practical and emotional. She is the one to kiss them goodnight, to soothe childhood hurts, and keep the family unit stable. I owe her a great debt. And I miss my family dearly when I am away.

Going away on a rescue deployment has become a greater challenge for me lately. Though my pre-teen daughters are becoming increasingly independent, my son is still deeply grounded in his parents, and he and I have a special father-son bond. We have patterns. When I am gone, that routine goes away. I know he misses it. I don't know if he understands how much I miss him, too. I feel pangs of emotion whenever I'm not able to kiss each of my kids goodnight.

When I come home, I love the welcome I get from my children. They make signs. They knock me down with their hugs. They jump straight into telling me every detail of what I've missed. It is blissful chaos.

And when I am home, I am truly, fully home. I don't have an office job to go to; my office is at home. I pick the kids up at the bus stop. I make them dinner. I attend swim meets and dance performances . . . until I get the next call.

I know my family is proud of my work. When I meet one of the kids' teachers or another parent, more often than not they've already heard child-enhanced stories about me. It should go without saying that my wife is my greatest supporter and the rock of our family.

I made a choice—before I got married or had children—to devote myself to animals. I don't question or second-guess that choice. It is simply who I am. Most people have a career. It's what they do. That's not me. My career is my life. This is the only job my kids have ever seen me do. My second daughter was born in June, and Hurricane Katrina happened two months later. I have been away for more than my share of holidays and birthdays—except for Christmas, which I have somehow always managed to spend at home, even if it meant briefly breaking off of a rescue deployment.

When I mentally catalogue all of those deployments, I also confront just how much I have punished my body. For years I have pushed myself, physically and emotionally, and I haven't taken adequate care of myself. The stresses related to animal rescues coupled with the manual labor and the contorted positions into which I often have to put myself have harmed my back and neck. I can't stand for lengthy periods of time, and I can't work at a desk. I am continually in some level of pain. Yet I don't allow myself to wallow in self-pity, which is a useless pursuit.

The one thing that soothes me—the one thing I do for myself and hope my children have adopted—is listening to music. From eight-track tapes in the car with my father to punk music to just about every genre today, music is a pillar of my life. I use music to set the tone or change the mood. I can't play an instrument or sing—which colleagues who took me to a karaoke bar learned after my rendition of Billy Idol's "Dancing With Myself." But I gain strength from music.

Music, animals, painting, and family have even made it into the tattoos I have on my body, which include, among others, my wife's name in script over my heart, Capone's paw print on my shoulder, and the Animal Rescue Corps logo on my forearm. I have the image of an early twentieth century Victrola phonograph above my right ankle. Coming from the horn are the words "Non, je ne regrette rien," the title of a song made famous in 1959 by jazz singer Edith Piaf, a favorite of mine. The words mean, "No, I regret nothing." There's a certain irony to that. The Victrola tattoo covered up an older tattoo, which was lettering I was told translated from a Chinese dialect as "vegan." Apparently there is no such word. That faux-vegan tattoo is one of my few regrets.

When I got clean, on December 13, 1988, the punk scene was fading. But one of the first things I remember being told in recovery was that everything I knew, everyone I hung out with, and all of the places I had hung out were no longer. I was told I would likely need to move. Everything had to be replaced with places of recovery. So I departed the punk scene, which led me to embrace other forms of music and other artists. Mostly it was jazz, old jazz, but I was open to anything and everything. The singers I listened to—Billie Holliday, Johnny Cash, Nina Simone, Leonard Cohen, Bob Dylan, Edith Piaf—were all about emotions I was working to connect with. They sang of sorrow, and their work helped me process mine.

When I lived in the Bay Area, I would get lost in the aisles of Amoeba Records, a huge store where you could find almost any used album you wanted to find. I recall coming across a copy of

The Dead Kennedy's album *Holiday in Cambodia*. After picking that up, I found myself picking up copies of old punk records I hadn't listened to in a decade or so. I remember questioning myself: *Do I want to bring this back into my life?* At home, I quickly made a mix tape on cassette, and I reconnected—from a now safe place of time and continued recovery—with a key part of my past.

Of all the musicians I have listened to, occasionally met and befriended, I still particularly treasure one deep, if fleeting, relationship.

Jeff Buckley was a cult figure in American music, a gifted singer, songwriter, and guitarist whose greatest fame arrived after his death in 1997. Buckley is most known for his haunting cover of the Leonard Cohen song, "Hallelujah." Now recorded by countless others, its opening lines are familiar to millions: "Now I've heard there was a secret chord; That David played, and it pleased the Lord; But you don't really care for music, do you?"

When Buckley's *Grace*, his only studio album, came out in 1994, I was nearing the end of my first stint at the Washington Humane Society. I had two roommates who worked for BMG, the music rights management company. Because of where they worked, we often had new music to listen to, and they frequently had concert tickets and backstage passes to share.

I remember that they had brought home a copy of *Grace*, which they listened to over and over, all the while chatting about the good-looking singer with the dreamy eyes. I never paid a great deal of attention. It was background music in our house. Exactly why, I don't know, but when they invited me to a Jeff Buckley show at Washington's legendary 9:30 Club, including passes to a pre-show and an after-show, I accepted the offer.

The pre-party was at a Cajun-themed restaurant. It had a pool table. I was pretty good at pool so I put my four quarters down to signify I wanted to play the winner of the game in progress. I wound up playing against—and beating—the singer from the opening act. During the game I noticed from the corner of my eye when Buckley put his quarters on the table, and he became my next opponent. As we played, we started chatting, and we immediately hit it off. He was fascinated by my work and peppered me with questions about animals and animal rescue. I won the game, Buckley headed back to the party, and I continued to take on new challengers. A few games later, Buckley came for another turn. We continued the conversation. It wasn't as if I was talking to a celebrity; he was just a fascinating person, and one who had a spark of understanding and compassion about him. We discovered we had grown up near each other, at about the same time. We talked about punk rock and decided we had probably been to some of the same shows. In a remarkably short time, he stopped being "Buckley" and became Jeff to me. As someone who has relatively few male friends, it was a welcome instant relationship.

Jeff had a show to do, so he left. Listening to him perform to the crowded house, I truly heard his music for the first time. It grabbed me. It affected me. It had an energy and a sorrow, too, especially when he did a cover of one of my favorite Nina Simone songs, "Lilac Wine." It was magical.

We went backstage after the show, talked to Jeff a little more, said some thank yous and goodbyes. But now, Jeff wasn't the guy I'd played pool with a few hours ago; he was an artist, and an artist who was interested in my work.

We didn't exchange phone numbers. It was just an instant friendship that seemed to end in an instant.

Months later, after my move to New York, I was in Greenwich Village at a restaurant called The Flying Burrito when Jeff walked in. Our eyes met, he looked at me and said, "Animal cop." He sat down. We chatted for a bit, and this time we exchanged phone numbers.

We got together shortly after that, at The Flying Burrito. It turned out almost all of our conversation that night was again about me. Beside his interest in animal welfare, he was particularly interested in learning about a vegan way of life. It seemed to be something he was contemplating, and he was looking for a guide. We met again after his Australian tour, and maybe a time or two more. It was a brief relationship based on genuine respect.

Jeff drowned in the Wolf River in Memphis, Tennessee, where he was developing his second album, in 1997. By then, I was living in San Francisco. I had recently called him, to find his number had been disconnected. I soon learned why.

Jeff was an artist I came to respect greatly, and a friend I still miss. Although we met only a few times, Jeff's friendship was, for me, surprisingly deep. It saddens me to this day that none of us will hear any new music from Jeff—and that I will never get to share his companionship again. It was more, though. Jeff was intensely creative. He used notes and lyrics to capture moments, tell stories, and convey deep emotion. He thought, wrote, and performed like no one else. And through our conversations—and from his example—I learned new facets of leadership. Rescuing animals often demands quick thinking in dicey situations, and leading animal rescues requires persuasion, the channeling of emotion, and creative thinking. Like a singer standing alone in a spotlight in the middle of a stage, I came to learn that being a leader in my field meant figuring out how to be visible and vulnerable on my own kind of stage.

CHAPTER FIFTEEN

LIES AND LOVE

When Animal Rescue Corps posts photos and videos on social media that document our rescue operations, we know they will elicit strong emotional responses that stretch well beyond our team on the ground. People who are distressed by pictures of suffering animals being rescued from horrible conditions often direct angry words toward the individuals responsible, sometimes calling for violence against them, demanding the publication of their names and addresses. That is not a sentiment I support.

ARC's staff and volunteers feel and care deeply about the animals and communities we serve. We are well acquainted with feelings of foreboding, anxiety, and sadness as a rescue operation begins, and the tears flow freely at our emergency shelters. But I try to steer away from anger and retribution. That is why we allow the justice system to do its work. Vengeance directed toward a puppy mill owner or an animal hoarder is simply not productive. Anger does not help animals, nor does it enhance a community.

On every rescue deployment, we are aware that our work also incites an inflammatory response from a small cadre of detractors, people who believe animals are mere property from which to profit. They claim we are "terrorists" or "vigilantes" who steal animals and people's livelihoods, acting outside of and above the law. Many zero in on me in the vilest possible manner, going so far as to advocate a "Second Amendment solution" if I ever come near their property.

Being attacked is never pleasant, but I work to stay above the fray. Addressing violence with violence or volleying incendiary language back and forth helps no one and solves nothing. Espousing negativity does not end suffering or inspire compassion. It perpetuates negative stereotypes of animal advocates, thereby diminishing us—and our movement. That kind of behavior is the antithesis of everything we stand for.

Hand in hand with compassion is my belief in, and commitment to, justice. Direct verbal or physical confrontation with those who do harm is about vengeance, not justice. Vengeance does nothing to change the way people think about animals or further our cause. Our justice system, like any system, may have shortcomings, but the system and our law enforcement partners are the greatest tools we have. Utilizing the judicial process, coupled with a structured operation and compassion, is the most effective way to directly address animal cruelty and create a lasting solution. This means supporting our law enforcement partners who are doing everything within their power to ensure an individual responsible for animal cruelty does not abuse animals in the future. Our justice system's triumph over vengeance and vigilantism is one of the most vital traits of our civil society. While I believe that society as a whole is evolving and becoming more compassionate, more aware, and more accepting than ever before, we are still very much living in the time of the tabloid, a time when individuals, industries, and fringe elements in the news media thrive by spreading misinformation and inspiring dissension, hate, and ill-will.

Working at the request of law enforcement partners, Animal Rescue Corps is charged with removing and caring for people's "property," and the evidence we gather frequently leads to criminal charges of animal cruelty. Sadly, some special interest groups and industries that profit from animal suffering attack ARC and other animal protection organizations for violating property rights and even the Constitution, ignoring the fact that we are operating as an agent of the local authorities. They use over-the-top language and, driven by their agenda to discredit us and distract from the real issues, fabricate stories, launch personal attacks, and tell lies. These entities are simply trying to defend something that has no defense. Their incendiary words do not excuse cruelty, and their assertions that our actions are illegal are unconvincing at best and often so ridiculous they immediately discredit themselves.

Repeating or refuting their ludicrous allegations only serves to perpetuate them. I choose not to stoke that fire. By drawing from our foundation of compassion, we do not allow the misguided and derogatory words of others to detract from our work. We are fighting for the animals, but we are also fighting for the society we want to see.

Empathetic, compassionate people who fight for justice carry enough of a burden. We must not allow our compassion for animals to be channeled into hate for people. I see this happen within our movement, when one rescuer or advocate decides that another is not saving or advocating for animals the "right way." This is more regrettable than the hate propagated by the individuals and industries profiting from animal suffering. Together, and only together, we can remove the stain on society created by animal abuse by demonstrating that compassion has no boundaries and every living being is deserving of our consideration.

Getting into the fray with detractors would mean I was doing a disservice to our amazing volunteers, who are the true heart of ARC. They are committed to any task and are some of the most positive, committed people I will ever meet. We have veterinarians who volunteer their time and skills to care for animals desperately in need of medical attention. We have groomers who take gnarled masses of fur and nails and turn them back into recognizable dogs. We have a remarkable group of creative individuals who volunteer their talents to visually document and communicate the lifesaving work ARC does so that others can connect with our mission.

We have people who turn an empty warehouse into a functioning shelter. We have people who feed and clean. We have people who deliver supplies. We have people who generously support us financially. We have people across North America volunteering their time and vehicles to transport animals from rescue operations to our incredibly hard-working placement partners where their journey to a home begins.

ARC's volunteers differ greatly in age, background, experience, skills, and physical abilities, but all of our volunteers are united by a singular motivation: to save lives. When called, ARC volunteers do not hesitate to put their lives on hold to come to the aid of abused and neglected animals. The work is not easy or glamorous, and they receive no paychecks. They are rewarded simply, yet profoundly, by witnessing the animals they've worked to save reclaim the lives that had been stolen from them.

"People ask me why I volunteer at ARC," wrote Connie Irwin of Nashville. Her answer is stirring. "I often tell them that I am making a difference in my community. You will never find a more grateful and accepting comrade than an animal you have comforted. I have made a lot of new friends, and not just the four-legged kind. Working side by side with strangers who share similar interests can form lifetime friendships. I have discovered skills that I never knew I had and have been surprised at what I am capable of achieving."

When I think of ARC's volunteers, I find myself humbled. I am astonished by how much they do, how much they care, and how much they propel me to continue our work. They inspire me beyond expression. They do not merely embody the goals of ARC. They are its heart, its soul, and its greatest reason to hope and to be hopeful.

I also have been fortunate to have, in Tim Woodward, Karla Goodson, and Michael Cunningham, an outstanding group of founding members of ARC, and I return to them here in tribute to their hard work and dedication.

Karla, Tim, and Michael simply want to get things done. They have been driving forces of our organization, but have chosen to lead in subtle ways. They use their talents for the betterment of animals, yet they don't seek attention.

When I speak on behalf of ARC, when I am in the media spotlight, or when some of our supporters put me on a pedestal, Karla, Tim, and Michael see me as who I am. They keep me grounded. They keep me honest. Even in the most trying situations, there is safety in their company. When I am looking to make a challenging decision, I seek their counsel. And they never hesitate to make jokes at my expense. Having that level of trust in anyone is a rarity.

Tim is an extraordinary communicator. He is capable of seeing an issue from all angles before he formulates a well-reasoned opinion. He opens me to new perspectives. There are even situations in which I find myself asking what Tim would do.

When Tim joined me to create ARC, he brought along Michael and we have all benefitted. His work and his work ethic are vital to our mission. As I have watched Tim and Michael as a couple, I can say I have never seen two people with such a keen sense of family. Their care—for each other and for others around them—has taught me much about the true meaning of family values.

CHAPTER SIXTEEN

MISSISSIPPI BLUES

None of us likes to fail. Falling short is not in our nature. Most of us have an innate drive to succeed, to work around difficulties, to persevere, and to finish what we started, even in situations in which success has eluded our grasp due to circumstances beyond our control.

For me, moving on from a situation in which a case can't be made for action against an animal abuser is a significant challenge. Sometimes we can't close a puppy mill because law enforcement does not consider conditions to be sufficient for a cruelty case or any other kind of case to proceed. To be sure, I see no benefit to society from large-scale puppy breeding operations of any variety. Even if a breeding operation is hygienic, where animals get proper water, nutrition, and veterinary care, a world with so many unwanted animals does not need more purebred companion animals. We do not need more animals in steel-barred cages; we do not need more lives created to satisfy human vanity—especially when shelters are full of highly adoptable cats and dogs. Puppy mills, whether or not their operations are "legal," are inhumane by definition. However, the work of Animal Rescue Corps is not based on what I believe is right or wrong. We document crimes against animals; we work within the justice system to end inhumane, illegal conditions and work with authorities to create a lasting solution; we closely cooperate with local law enforcement officials and prosecutors to help them make a legal case. Animal cruelty cases must not be a matter of my perception. They must be legally legitimate—and the evidence must be sufficient.

The case in Mississippi, which I discussed in chapter two, is an excellent case in point. It was, in my estimation, an unacceptable situation. However, neither the sheriff's department nor I, our attorney, or our veterinarian could marshal the justification to seize the cats, dogs, or horses. As much as I believed animals were suffering, we just couldn't legally remove them.

Since that day, we stayed in contact with the Union County director of animal control, Curt Clayton, who was determined to end the suffering on the property. But there had been no further developments.

Just shy of two years after our visit, everything changed.

In July 2015, one of the property's owners walked into the office of a local veterinarian with a dog by her side. Approximately three years old, the female golden retriever had ticks and fleas throughout her body. She was, the doctor reported, severely emaciated, dehydrated, and in organ failure. And she was pregnant. A picture of her, taken after fleas and ticks had been removed, showed sunken, lifeless eyes due, the doctor said, to malnutrition. The property owner told the veterinarian's staff that she wanted the dog cut open and the puppies removed so she could sell them. She professed she didn't care if the mother survived or died during the process. The woman claimed to have another dog at home in similar circumstances. The golden retriever, too weak to stand, gave birth the following day to a litter of dead puppies.

Thankfully, the veterinarian's office called the sheriff's office, and the sheriff's department immediately called ARC. This time, based on that single, severely damaged dog, we would have a case.

It was late in the afternoon on Monday when the sheriff's department contacted us and forwarded the veterinarian's photograph of the dog. The sheriff had, by then, sent a deputy to secure the property, and the initial reports from the field were dire. This would be a race-to-the-scene rescue emergency.

The information we had was far from comprehensive, but it was immediately obvious that our challenges would be stiff. We would have to rescue animals not from the one property I had visited two years before, but from two properties: the owners' house and another property of theirs that was mainly made up of open fields. We would have dogs, cats, horses, and donkeys. And we would be in the middle of Mississippi in the middle of July. This rescue presented conditions—weather, terrain, and multiple locations—that greatly increased the difficulty of the operation.

My team from ARC got very busy, very quickly. The properties were in Blue Springs in Union County, about a ninety minute drive southeast from Memphis, Tennessee, and about four hours from Jackson, Mississippi. Our emergency shelter would be in a warehouse space in Tunica, Mississippi, a casino town to the northwest, about twenty miles from Memphis. We partnered with equine rescue groups that could jump into action. Our team in Tennessee rented a box truck and began loading cages, tents, tables, and medical supplies. Teams of volunteers from Virginia, Maryland, Washington, DC, and even Canada made rapid preparations for travel. Tim and Michael loaded ARC's mobile command post full of supplies and prepared to hit the road.

It bears mentioning that this deployment was the first since Michael had become the fourth staff member of ARC, joining the team as our public information officer, a role he has served in as a volunteer since our inception. Although Michael had long been a *de facto* ARC staff member, it was a great pleasure to recognize his hard work by formally bringing him on the payroll. Michael does a superb job of balancing transparency with journalists against the fact that most of our work is on crime scenes.

This deployment also came just weeks after my wife and I (and Chicago) had the pleasure and honor of joining Tim and Michael on the steps of the United States Supreme Court, as the justices handed down their historic decision on marriage equality. Being there when our country finally achieved this one hurdle of equal rights was a stirring moment. Knowing what this historic moment in human rights meant to dear friends and the future of America made it indelible.

Michael and Tim drove all night to get to Blue Springs.

On Tuesday, just twenty-four hours after the first call from the sheriff's department, Karla and I get on a plane to Memphis. There, we rendezvous with co-author Rich, and after a vegan barbecue dinner, capped by a memorable vegan banana cream pie, we drive to Union County, where we meet up with Kim Rezac, Amy Haverstick, and Amiee Stubbs.

At five o'clock on Wednesday morning, I get ready by spraying myself from neck to ankles with bug spray and then spraying again on top of my clothes and boots. The hotel room is saturated with a mildly unpleasant, slightly perfumed chemical odor, but the protection is worth the smell. We have plenty of experience telling us that these kind of properties will be full of ticks, fleas, and chiggers.

We roll our small caravan to the sheriff's office, a parking lot still familiar from two years before. The equine rescue teams and their trailers soon join us, along with a team from the Mississippi State University College of Veterinary Medicine, and we pile in behind the sheriff and his team. We drive just a few miles to the same staging area we had used two years ago, a patch of asphalt and gravel surrounded by fields of invasive Kudzu vines alongside several converging highways. Escorted by officers, my assessment team breaks off and heads to the first property in a pickup truck. Our destination turns out to be nothing but the intersection of a narrow road with a dirt path. It is barely seven o'clock, but the temperature has already eclipsed eighty degrees.

In addition to the heat and humidity—the heat index will top 105—we face daunting conditions. This first property, much of which is open, overgrown fields, is accessible only by a quarter-mile long, muddy dirt path with a steep hill and precipitous drop-off to one side. Our intake area will have to be at the bottom of the hill. We also learn that the second parcel of land we must clear of suffering animals, surrounding the family's house, is not accessible from this location. We will have to finish here, move the entire operation, unload, and start over.

Once everyone in the exploratory wave has reached the summit, we step out into vegetation that is knee high or greater, surrounding a ramshackle barn. With horse stalls on one side, enclosed space on the other, and a breezeway in the middle, this structure might once have been practical, usable space on a working farm. When I visited this property two years ago, the enclosed spaces had family members living in them. What we find now is crumbling, with junk strewn all about: a ripped-to-pieces recliner on one side, its companion love seat on the other. In between are bits and pieces of lumber and building materials, along with empty bags of horse feed. From one of the enclosed rooms of the barn we can hear barking.

Karla and I head off in the all-terrain vehicles with a couple of deputies and Dr. Uri Donnett, a resident from Mississippi State and our veterinarian for the day, to survey the rest of the property. We already know we will be finding dogs running free, in chain-link enclosures, and in the barn, where there are cats, too.

Rich, Kim, and several others wait at the barn. A few minutes later, Kim notices something moving near the breezeway. She can see rustling but not what is underneath the brush. Approaching slowly and cautiously, Kim reaches in and pulls out a puppy. Floppy-eared, tan colored, and possibly a golden retriever, his most notable feature is a patch of black fur just under his left eye. He is in pain. Just a quick glance shows why. His chest and belly are dotted every half inch or so by ticks. Highways of fleas march around them. The inner flaps of his ears are covered by dozens, if not hundreds, more ticks. His toes are grotesquely pushed apart because of the number of ticks between each digit. He is lethargic and extremely dehydrated. He is our first rescue of the day, a first rescue who needs medical care—and fast.

Kim places the puppy in the bed of one of the deputy's trucks. As soon as he returns, Dr. Donnett jumps in to make a cursory evaluation as Kim tries to get the puppy to take a drink of water. A quick examination reveals the obvious: Dr. Donnett confirms that this puppy needs immediate care to save his life—in a veterinary hospital where he may possibly require a blood transfusion. The infestations on his body have sapped the dog that much. By now, as the initial assessment of the property continues, it is mid-morning; the sun is high in the sky and the temperature is approaching triple digits. To give the puppy just a bit of shade, Dr. Donnett removes his Pepto-Bismol-colored surgical scrub top and drapes it over the corner of the pickup truck bed. He has a deputy drive him to the bottom of the hill and the shade—and the medical equipment—of the examination table. The doctor looks more closely at the dog and checks vital signs. His initial evaluation is confirmed. In a matter of minutes, a volunteer heads for the animal hospital. Against the odds, the puppy lives. For our team, the gravity of the situation we will confront all day becomes that much more real.

As always, we operate under a command chart. I will lead the extraction team and be the primary handler for dogs and cats. This is a somewhat unusual circumstance because we also have an equine extraction team, which will handle all of the horses and donkeys. Karla, per usual, will take charge of the intake and evidence tables. We are fortunate to have Ada Dever as our emergency shelter manager. Ada is one of the newer members of our team. She came to us through one of our Basic Animal Rescue Course sessions. Working with ARC, Ada developed a reputation as a strong worker and as a dedicated shelter manager. She leads people well, is highly regarded by volunteers, and manages the largest contingent of volunteers on our rescues.

It's time to kick this rescue into gear. Back at the top of the hill, a truck pulling a flatbed trailer delivers about a dozen cages. I find a loose black Lab who seems to have trouble standing, and then I move into the barn. To the left, I enter through a small, unfinished room with a bowl of filthy water and some old, stale kibble strewn across the floor—but no animals. That room leads to a larger space, equally rustic, full of cats. The dilapidated particle board walls have absorbed bacteria, stench, and disease. There is no air flow, just a closed room with stifling heat. We remove all of the cats we can, but a number of them have, by now, scurried into spaces in the walls. We leave humane traps behind for them and have our trapping team monitor them throughout the day. The dog side of the barn is notable for how still it is. When you step into a room containing two dozen dogs, you expect considerable activity—at least barking. These dogs lie listless behind and under furniture—a couch, a chair, a television stand, and an old TV—that we have to remove first to get access to them. None of the dogs scatter; they don't even move. They were smart enough to know that moving would exhaust them further, making a terrible situation even worse. There is no water inside; just a non-functional, dry toilet. When I begin removing the dogs, it immediately became clear that their conditions—ticks, fleas, and all manner of decay and conditions of neglect—are at least as bad as the puppy Kim had found a few minutes before. The neglect of these animals is vastly worse than what we had seen on our first visit.

With a cursory glance, I see that at least one of the dogs I just removed is going to need immediate care. Back outside, another loose dog wanders up to us, an adult Weimaraner whose neck is completely obscured by a blanket of ticks.

It is painfully obvious that even standing still in these conditions will be taxing. Staying hydrated is a losing battle. This is going to be a longer, tougher day than any of us could have estimated, and neither I, nor anyone on the team, will be at peak efficiency. We feel weary from just the first batch of rescues. The trip down the hill with a flatbed full of cages is even slower than the ascent, and we bask in even those few minutes of cool air. The intake team jumps into action but is also not able to work at optimal speed. We have several air-conditioned vehicles standing by, including our

ARC command center and an ambulance the sheriff's department has brought to the scene. I urge people to spend time in the cooling stations, and I take my own advice as often as possible. As the day wears on, none of it works sufficiently. Yet no one on the team wants to quit. The spirit of compassion is as strong as ever, even if our bodies are taxed. We all realize that no matter how we feel at the moment, our discomfort will be short-lived. These animals have no refuge. They simply suffer—day after day.

During much of the morning, the male property owner is on the scene, pacing back and forth in front of the driveway near our assessment area. Later, as his teenage son joins him, deputies take them up the hill to have a look and retrieve some paperwork from another building. The son assists us in picking up a handful of dogs that are running free, including a black Lab he calls Blizzard and a Great Pyrenees.

Our rescues at the top of the hill become more spread out, and the conditions for the remaining dogs are ever worse. The lucky ones, in structures that seem to be held together by sheer will, have sheets of wood above their heads, offering at least some shade. Another Lab is one of the first we get to, his cage ironically notable because an ancient window unit air conditioner sits on top of his enclosure, holding down the sheet of wood that acts as a roof.

Farther back on the property, two German Shepherds are living in conditions sadly typical of several other dogs. Their enclosure is relatively spacious, perhaps ten feet by ten feet, the walls made of rusted chain link fence about six feet high. There are patches in the fence, and there are broken spots. One of the dogs sticks his head through to peer out. The floor is made of brick, which is absorbing every bit of the sun's rays. There is no roof, save for two small pieces of wood attached precariously at two of the corners. There are two igloo-shaped doghouses, neither of which looks large enough to reasonably hold either dog. A couple of large buckets hold what is certainly by now very warm water. As if we didn't have enough evidence these dogs have been neglected, the gate on the enclosure is virtually rusted shut. They have been in this prison for a long time. To get them out, we have to peel the metal gate open. These dogs, hot, tired, hungry, and thirsty, are as stoically docile as the dogs in the barn had been.

More enclosures dot the property, and we work our way through each. The pace feels agonizingly slow, but I can only imagine what it must be like for the dogs.

In a parallel operation, the equine rescue team is hard at work gathering horses and loading them onto trailers. They, too, have some cases that will require immediate medical attention. One bay horse, who has many skin lesions, has what appears to be a bullet hole in her neck. You can look right through it. A severely sunburned light-colored foal is so emaciated her ribs jut out in waves, her bone structure plainly visible, her spirit nowhere in evidence.

Slowly and unsteadily, we complete our rescues on the first property. With dogs running free in such an overgrown area, it is not possible to say we have gotten every one, but to the best of our knowledge, the area is clear.

It feels like the end of a very long day, but ours is just half over. We pack up everything—cages, tables, tents, and medical equipment—and drive just a few miles to the second property, which will be a very different situation. The distance from field locations to intake tents will be just steps. Shade and shelter will always be nearby. The family's home is here.

The house sits back around 500 feet, down a dirt-and-gravel driveway. It's a single story dwelling that, like the driveway, has seen better days. With cream-colored aluminum siding and green shutters, the most notable feature is a front porch, its railings wrapped in wide-spaced metal fencing material, with bags of horse feed and bales of hay on its unfinished decking-board floor. One of the front windows is boarded up. To the right of the house are horse pens. Donkeys wander at will around the property and come right up to members of our group. A couple pieces of frameless metal fencing material create a *de facto* gate at the edge of the road, the only thing keeping the donkeys enclosed. In front of the house, on the opposite side of the driveway, stands a single-wide house trailer and a carport with a series of pens under its roof, one containing a bunch of squirming Weimaraner puppies. On the back of the house is another enclosed porch, this one with seven blonde puppies and their mother peeking out.

The rescues on this property are vastly simpler, and the process moves much more rapidly. We will leave the house and the equines—and the special challenges they represent—for last. The family is home and inside; the horses, more than we had estimated, are greater than our capacity to transport them.

We begin with several loose dogs and then get the Weimaraner puppies from the pens in front. With that sweep, the intake and assessment tables are at capacity for a bit. The dogs have to sit outside in crates for longer than we would like; however, they are closely monitored and put in air-conditioned transport vehicles as quickly as possible. Once full, each transport begins the two-hour-plus drive to the emergency shelter. The puppies from the back porch create another capacity crowd for assessment.

By now it is pushing on to evening, and the interior of the house remains. I notice one of the children emerge from the front with a dog on a leash. I grab Rich and ask him to keep his eyes on that situation. She methodically walks one dog and another, until the count reaches nine. They are all adults, and quite clearly are breeding mothers, so engorged that their abdomens nearly scrape the ground. The girl's affection for them is obvious.

Entering the house is a delicate situation. Whatever the circumstances may be, this is a family's home and there are children present. I want as few of my people in the house as possible, and I want them to move quickly, quietly, and respectfully. Because of the fact that it is a family's home, I will limit my description, save to say it is far from clean. A deputy precedes us, and we get to work.

There are more cats inside the house, whom we get out first. The breeding mother dogs are clustered under tables and around furniture. Getting them out is relatively simple, especially since they are used to being leashed. The puppies, too, are easy to move; they are clustered in plastic kiddie pools, one blue, one red.

By this time, daylight has faded, and we still have horses and donkeys to deal with. The intake and veterinary teams are processing the last of the dogs and cats, who will soon be on transports and off the property. Officer Clayton arrives back on the scene, towing an industrial sized generator-powered bank of floodlights. With a little tinkering, the engine lumbers to life, and we can see again.

Thanks to some persistence on the telephone, equine volunteers have located an additional large trailer that is on the way. Once that makes the scene, the vehicles with hooved rescues are loaded and head out. The rest of our team takes apart unused cages and collapses tents. The supply vehicles hit the road, as well.

While this is happening, I am behind closed doors with the sheriff and the property owners, attempting to negotiate the surrender of the animals. This discussion is arduous and takes nearly two hours, but I get a signed surrender of all of the animals. They now belong to ARC. We must treat them as evidence, since the local prosecutor must still consider whether to file criminal charges.

When I emerge, it is night. Karla is still there, as are Tim, Michael, and Rich. We all pile in the mobile command post and head for the staging area, where other vehicles are parked. On the way, we debate whether to make the drive to the emergency shelter or stay put for the night. Ultimately, we decide to stay. The hotel where we had stayed the previous night has rooms available. The drive there, all eight miles of it, feels eternal. And as we enjoy air conditioning and a chance to stop sweating, we all begin to feel the emotion of the day just past.

Whenever our team deploys, the days are long. Yet this one may have been our most brutal. I was not at my best, and the team members all struggled. Despite the conditions, we operated as a team. The right people did the right jobs, and the sum of our efforts is that we completed a job two years after we had first tried. But we did it. We kept a promise to more than a hundred animals that we would free them from neglect and squalor. Members of our team looked after each other so we could all look after them.

ARC remains a small operation with a big mission. Karla, Tim, Michael, and I cannot conduct large-scale rescue operations on our own. ARC is, as I designed it to be, an operation with volunteers at its core. I never cease to be touched when I see what that collective compassion can do. We tested the physical limits of that compassion in Blue Springs, Mississippi, but we never approached the limits of our team's determination to save lives.

Indeed, the compassion we practice depends on determination. If we change communities one at a time, we must have the drive to continue on to new places and new challenges. I have no doubt that Animal Rescue Corps is up to any challenge.

My own ride through life this far has also been driven by determination—to see each twist and turn as an opportunity to become wiser, a better leader, a more compassionate person. There remain lessons to be learned, animals to rescue, people and communities to educate, and missions not yet encountered, but I spend every day believing that the power of compassion is growing and unstoppable.

The decision to stay the night in Mississippi was a good one—and not just because a fatigue-induced car accident could have been in our future. We still have animals at two local emergency animal clinics that we need to pick up the next day. Only then will we be able to make the drive to witness, for the first time, the wonderful cacophony of our emergency shelter in Tunica.

When I get to my room at the end of a twenty-hour rescue day, as I fumble with the electronic key card to open the hotel room door, it dawns on me that this is the same room I stayed in the night before. As the door swings open, I am immediately hit by the lingering smell of bug spray. It's all for the best, though. Otherwise, it would smell like a puppy mill.

EPILOGUE

As I write these final words, it is December 24. The tree in our living room is decorated and aglow with lights and ornaments. The kids' presents are wrapped and hidden away. Late tonight, I will arrange them under the tree, knowing from past experience that the children will rise early on Christmas morning. For another year, the string of holidays I have been home to celebrate with my family will remain unbroken. But just barely.

In what we celebrate as a season of lights and giving and peaceful wishes, there are places where the abuse, suffering, and neglect of animals recognize no holiday season. In just the past few days, four of those places have emerged as potential rescue cases.

If these were standard cases, we would be working now to launch an investigation to take forward to local officials. But these are not standard cases; we do not have to build these cases. In each one, we have already been in contact with law enforcement agencies. These are clearly identified instances of cruelty, and it is time not to investigate but to act.

The first is an abandonment case involving a purported rescue group. The elderly woman who owned the facility is ill, has moved away, and is going into hospice care. She reportedly took about ten dogs with her and left behind about fifty—without food, water, or care, some running loose on the property, most penned up or in cages. She just packed up and left. The report on the situation came to law enforcement via the woman's daughter. The daughter forewarned a hospice nurse of the dogs with her mother, and happened to mention that she was concerned about the fifty left behind. By sheer coincidence, the hospice nurse volunteers in animal rescue. The nurse went to see the animals. She found one dead dog, one dying dog, and another who appeared to be in critical condition. The elderly woman's daughter permitted the nurse to take the dogs to a veterinary hospital, and she began calling around, looking for a group to help. We got the dying dog to one of our vets, someone who has experience dealing with animal neglect and abuse. ARC contacted law enforcement, which is working with us to secure a warrant. Until we can get on that property, the nurse and the daughter are working together to provide the dogs their most basic needs.

In the second situation, law enforcement has been on the scene of a suspected dogfighting case. An official called us, having witnessed the horrible plight of these animals without knowing what to do. He sent us pictures of a mother dog who was nothing but a skeleton, a bag of bones. One of her puppies lay dead next to her, and a second appeared to be barely clinging to life. He also sent pictures of the other pit bulls on chains, obviously scarred and beaten up. The question for me was whether to jump on a plane and deal with the situation—about half a dozen dogs, which is a typical quantity in a dogfighting operation. If the officers who were on the scene had to pull out, it would take a warrant to get back in, and the owner might have time to tamper with evidence or remove it altogether, including the remains of animals.

Fortunately, because of the relatively small number of animals, we have been able to call on Animal Rescue Corps partners, who have removed the dogs and transported them to safety. For me, it has been a delicate situation; being hundreds of miles away, I can advise, but I do not have the direct knowledge to assist in decision-making. ARC sent paperwork to our partners on how to execute a surrender. The suspected owner of the facility has been arrested. It seems everything has gone off without a hitch. However, before we could celebrate the lives saved, case number three came onto our radar.

An animal control department we have worked with before approached us about a hoarding case of around one hundred fifty dogs. The property owner is willing to surrender them. They are, by and large, not in great shape, but they are being provided some care—less than adequate, but some care. To the best of our knowledge, none is dead or dying.

Last night, we got a report from an animal control partner in the Midwest about a suspected puppy mill, our fourth case. It is a desperate situation. ARC is looking more deeply into the situation. The owner, it seems, has been off the grid for so long that no one in the animal welfare field has been aware of his operation. It's all Beagles, perhaps as many as eighty. As always, those estimates can vary wildly from what we find when we get there.

At the moment, we are triaging the situations. Our first consideration must be the condition of the animals—now or what we can predict about the near future. Simply put, are they dying?

We have to be smart and consider the expenses to the organization. I will never let financial resources dictate our response to suffering, but we also need to think ahead about costs and the fundraising we will need to do. I break things down into key questions. Do I have the people, the equipment, the emergency shelter? Is it likely we can get a warrant? Is law enforcement fully on board? Are cases grouped geographically? Will there be weather issues?

It's Christmas Eve, but my day has been dominated by conference calls about the four cases. When Tim, Karla, other members of the ARC leadership, and I talk, we have to remind each other which case we are currently discussing, lest anything get confused. I still have last-minute gifts to pick up, kids to drive to activities, and a holiday party to attend in a few hours.

Across ARC's volunteer network, I have a lot of people who are deeply invested in spending time over the holidays with their loved ones. I know they will jump into action if I ask them, but it would be a sacrifice. That is a sacrifice I have been willing to make, and my family has had to come to terms with it. I will be home for Christmas this year, but a day or two later, I may be on the road.

The fact remains that I shut down cruelty, and I negotiate with people who are unwilling to treat animals with respect and dignity. That can be a difficult path—not just for me, but for my organization and everyone everywhere who believes we can do better for animals. It heartens me to know that Animal Rescue Corps has a staff and a cadre of volunteers who will respond if we ask them. They will leave the comforts of home—the tree, a warm fire, a festive table, candles, lights, and their friends and family—to walk into a place of suffering and collectively say, "Your suffering ends today." Their compassion for those who cannot care for themselves sustains me. They inspire me. Their willingness to act is what continues to make me believe unwaveringly in a compassionate future, a future in which we value all lives.

A NOTE ABOUT THE COVER

The dog you see me pulling out of a cage on the cover of this book is now named Callie. She existed in that cage for eight years—without a name, without a family, and without hope. She was forced to breed litter after litter, outdoors during all weather conditions, on a puppy mill in rural Mississippi. She had never been to a veterinarian and had never been bathed or groomed. Her paws never connected with the earth; she languished in that wire-bottomed hutch in fear and loneliness day after day. After Callie's rescue by Animal Rescue Corps during Operation Autumn Angels on October 29, 2015, veterinarians diagnosed and treated her for severe anxiety, repetitive behaviors known as stereotypy, severe dental disease, infections in both ears, ear mites, and intestinal parasites. United Yorkie Rescue, one of ARC's valued placement partners, found a loving family in Dover, Tennessee, that adopted Callie. In their home for her remaining years, she will be met with nothing but love, patience, and the best of care.

ACKNOWLEDGMENTS

Tracy Reiman, a close friend for nearly thirty years, credits me for a moment when she believes I saved her life. What Tracy may not know is that she gave me my life. Tracy encouraged me and pushed me to join the field of animal protection. She launched what has become my quest to create a more compassionate society. Along that path, I have been honored to work with extraordinary, committed people dedicated to creating a world that values all life: leaders of change, selfless volunteers, open-hearted adopters, and many other extraordinary people. All of them have, by their examples, helped me continually strive toward the highest standards in animal rescue and protection. I am eternally grateful to Tracy and all the others who have followed, for guiding me and believing in me.

I consider myself a good writer, particularly when talking about the gift of compassion; however, I never considered myself the caliber of author who could write a book. Frankly, before this project, I had never even read an entire book. But I knew my story needed to be told with the intent to inspire others. I have been approached by many authors who wanted to write my story. But how could I let someone in? How could I trust someone to help me recount details of my life that I don't frequently discuss? My longtime friend Rich Folkers was the one I chose to trust. Thank you, Rich, for your perseverance, loyalty, and friendship.

We are fortunate in our lives to be graced by people who are like family, and I am grateful each day for the family of Animal

Rescue Corps. Even more rare are the people who are family. My wife and my kids support me, sustain me, and demonstrate to me daily that compassion is contagious and, once planted, will forever reach high.

Scotlund Haisley

Scotlund Haisley is a man of many facets: animal rescuer, leader, father, husband, artist, iconoclast, and friend. It has been my honor to become acquainted with them all. I treasure the time we spent developing the story on these pages. My wife, Elizabeth Mullen, is an invaluable adviser, conscience, and life partner—and a shining example of how good a dog trainer can be. My daughter Kelly is a trusted reviewer, and my daughter Christina a tough critic. This book owes a great debt to our agent, Josh Getzler, and our editor, Susan Randol. My work is influenced by a lifetime of four-legged family members—Max, Bear, Annie, Belle, Lily, Tess, Piper, Griffin, Cora, Lola, Guava, Perry, and Snowe—I have been proud to have in my life.

Richard Folkers